A Joy of Gardening

A Joy of Gardening

by V. Sackville-West

A Selection for Americans.

Edited by Hermine I. Popper.

HARPER & ROW, PUBLISHERS

New York, Hagerstown, San Francisco, London

N. Y.

c 1958.

Material in this book originally appeared in the books entitled *In Your Garden Again* and *More for Your Garden,* published in England.

ISBN: 0-06-013741-X

LIBRARY OF CONGRESS CATALOG CARD NUMBER: 76-39685

77 78 79 80 81 10 9 8 7 6 5 4 3 2 1

Contents

SUMMER

CONTENTS

AUTUMN

WINTER

CONTENTS

Editor's Preface

THE PLEASURES OF A GOOD garden book are much like those of a good cookbook. In both cases the reading can be done for its own sake, or to conjure up visions of future triumphs, or as a prod to immediate action. It is no accident that so many good gardeners are also good cooks: Both enjoy the aesthetic pleasure of a functional pursuit. Miss Sackville-West writes about gardening like a very good cook indeed.

Although these pieces were originally written by an Englishwoman about English gardens, this is a book for Americans. It is, in the first place, a prime example of a characteristically American enthusiasm, progressive education: It makes learning a pleasure, and its suggestive ideas tempt the reader inexorably on to learning by doing. England, moreover, is the source of our greatest gardening tradition, and of all the contemporary English writers about gardening none is more justly admired for her vision, style, and good sense than the writer whose London *Observer* articles are signed V. Sackville-West. Chiefly, however, the reason for bringing *A Joy of Gardening* to Americans is that the gardens of the two nations resemble each other more closely than most people realize. This is true not only of the herbaceous borders and rock gardens that our British ancestors carried across the ocean along with their language and their law. It is true, as well, of the many trees and shrubs that flourish on both sides of the Atlantic. It is true of the enemies that attack them. Above all, it is true of the shape and pattern of the well-built garden, the architecture of plants about which Miss Sackville-West writes so eloquently.

Of course there are differences—more moisture in England, for example, and generally narrower extremes of temperature. And these differences account for certain variations in method and result, for certain limitations in the mutual use of plant materials, for certain discrepancies in matters of time. But in terms of range—which is the only judicious term to use in connection with horticulture —it is safe to say that the British climate resembles that of the East Central Seaboard and Northwest States more closely than those resemble their neighbor states in the semi-tropical south and the icebound north. And the area of tolerance for British plants here spreads far beyond these boundaries. Nor is the traffic one way: Many American natives have traveled east to find a second home in England.

It has been possible, therefore, with a minimum of alterations to assemble from Miss Sackville-West's perceptive essays on gardening a selection of pertinence to large portions of the United States. Priority of choice has gone to those pieces that would be of interest in all parts of the country. Where exceptions exist—such as plant materials that cannot survive northern winters—internal evidence should reveal the fact to the reader. The regional bias of an editor whose gardening life has been spent in the northeast is perhaps inevitable; but an earnest effort has been made to hold it in check.

Anyone who wants to put Miss Sackville-West's precepts to action—and anyone who *doesn't* has stronger powers of resistance than the editor—would do well to refer to a good garden encyclopedia for details about hardiness and special cultural requirements. Taylor's *Encyclopedia of Gardening*, Bailey's *Manual of Cultivated Plants*, Rehder's *Manual of Cultivated Trees and Shrubs*, the American Rose Society's *Modern Roses*, and the Massachusetts Horticultural Society's *Plant Buyer's Guide* have all been invaluable in determining that no plant material has been discussed in this book that is not to be found somewhere in the United States. Miss Elizabeth Hall, of the New York Botanical Garden, and her assistant Mrs. Alletta Fredericks, have made what might have been a tortuous research chore a simple delight by their resourceful guidance through the library shelves. Special thanks are due to T. H. Everett, Horticulturist of that Garden, for bringing his voluminous knowledge of both the English and the American way of gardening to play on the manuscript.

Many of the differences in the gardens of the two nations are actually matters of habit—old customs and short memories that lead us to plant certain things, to place certain plants in juxtaposition, and to overlook other equally felicitous materials and patterns. If this book revives some forgotten images, and stimulates American gardeners to new enterprise, it will have served its purpose well. In any case, it cannot fail to bring pleasure.

White Plains, N. Y. H. I. P.

Spring

The beginnings of revival

THE FIRST MONTHS of the New Year can be the most unpleasant months in the calendar but they do bring some consolation in the beginnings of revival. Crocuses and other small bulbs appear, miraculous and welcome; they are apt, however, to leave a blank after they have died down, and it is for that reason that I suggest overplanting them with some little shrubs which will flower soon after.

I visualize a low bank or slope of ground, not necessarily more than two or three feet high, perhaps bordering some rough steps on a curve. You stuff and cram the bank with early-flowering bulbs, making a gay chintz-like or porcelain effect with their bright colors in yellow, blue, white, orange, red. Amongst these, you plant the little shrubs I want to recommend. *Corylopsis spicata* and *Corylopsis paucifolia* are two of the prettiest and softest, hung with yellow moths of flowers all along their twiggy branches. They are natives of Japan, and are related to the witchhazels. They seldom grow more than four feet high and about as much through; they need no pruning, and are graceful in their growth, pale as a primrose, and as early. Another little companion shrub on the bank would be *Forsythia ovata*. The big bushy forsythia is well known, but this small relation from Korea is not so often seen. It is perfectly hardy, and makes a tiny tree three to four feet high, flowering into the familiar golden blossoms, a golden rain pouring down in companionship with the *Corylopsis* after the bulbs have died away.

If you have room in your garden at the top of the bank or slope, I would urge you to plant *Cornus mas*, the Cornelian cherry. This cornel or dogwood produces its yellow flowers early, and is one of the best flowerers for forcing indoors. A big full-grown tree of *Cornus mas* is a sight to be seen, as I once saw one growing in a wood in Kent. It towered up fifteen feet and more, smothered in its myriads of tiny clusters, each individual flower-head like a bunch of snipped ribbons. If at first it seems a little disappointing and makes only a thin show, do not be discouraged, for it improves yearly with age and size, and one year will suddenly surprise you by the wealth of its blossom. It also produces long scarlet berries which you can, if you wish, eat.

A thin little grove

THERE IS OFTEN a strip of ground in a garden which cannot be put to good purpose without more labor than we can devote to it. It may once have been a lawn, which means mowing; or a long border, which needs weeding and upkeep; or merely a strip along the boundary fence in the garden of a new house, hitherto uncultivated, which demands some treatment to turn it into something better than a rough waste. I had an idea for such a place, which should be both pretty and labor-saving.

The shape does not matter so very much; it could be rectangular, square, or even circular, though I fancy a long narrow rectangle would give the best effect. What is important is that it should be *flat*, and that the ground surface should be level. No bumps; no depressions. You then plant it at regular intervals (say fifteen feet apart either way) with young stripling sapling trees, straight of stem and twiggy of head; it will be important to keep the stems clean of growth so that you can always see through and between them. A thin little grove is what I have in mind. The silver birch with its pale bark would be ideal, especially in a light or sandy soil; the linden, for any soil; the whitebeam, whose underside leaves show silver in the breeze; and even young oaks, round-topped and grown as standards.

The question will then arise of what you plant underneath. Since the heads of the little trees will be very green, the accent should be on emphasizing the greenness. Turf is probably impossible, because of the mowing, and anyway I think one should aim at a brighter green than that. I have a great weakness for sweet woodruff; it does not object to shade, it remains green from April until the autumn, it can be grown from seed, and it would make a dense cushion rather like those enormous eiderdowns (*duvets*) that one finds in old-fashioned French hotels. I would also plant some patches of greenish flowers; for instance, the green and silver star of Bethlehem; the wood anemone; lily of the valley; and, for later in the year, some clumps of Solomon's seal and the sweet-smelling *Smilacina racemosa*. I am not quite sure about these last two: they might be too tall, and might interrupt the vistas between the straight little trunks. Obviously such planting must depend upon individual taste, but of one thing I feel sure: that all color must be excluded. It must all be green and white; cool, symmetrical, and severe.

Woodland things

THE DOGTOOTH VIOLETS should now be coming into flower, so this is the time to study these curly objects and to decide if you would like to order some for planting next autumn. There will probably be a fine display of them at the flower shows. Of course one must expect everything to look better at a show than it will ever look in one's own garden. The exhibitors have chosen their best specimens and have arranged them in a very becoming bed of moist dark-brown-velvet peat moss, showing them up to their best advantage.

The dogtooth violets should be there, beneath the great flowering cherries and almonds of the spring. They are small, they are low, they are humble in stature, not more than six inches high, but with their beautifully mottled leaves and reflexed petals like tiny martagon lilies they are more than worthy of their place. Some of them are natives of central Europe, some of North America; they belong to the lily family and have nothing to do with violets. "Dogtooth" is because of the tuber, which is white and pointed like a fang. They prefer a little shade; light woodland is ideal for them; they like some sand and peat moss or leaf mold in their soil, which should be moist but never waterlogged; they dislike being moved, so leave them alone for years once they have settled down. I have seen them flourishing and increasing even under beech trees, where few things will grow. You can get them in white, pink, purple, and yellow.

The trilliums, or North American wood lilies, also called the trinity flowers from their triangular shape, flower a little later but enjoy the same conditions of shade and soil. Claret-colored, pink, or white, they grow to about a foot high and have the advantage of lasting a very long time, which seems to be true of most woodland things, I suppose because they do not get burnt up by a hot sun. The trilliums are very striking, and a group of only three or four makes quite an effect. They, as well as the dogtooth violets, are ideal not only for woodland planting but also for a cool shaded place in a rock garden.

The claret-colored one is *Trillium erectum*, the pink, *Trillium stylosum*. The white one is *Trillium grandiflorum*, which in its native home is known as wake robin, a name we commonly give to our wild arum or lords-and-ladies.

Pans of bright flowers

AT THIS TIME of year, or even earlier, a few pans of small, brightly colored flowers give vast pleasure. No need to be ambitious, for even half a dozen pans on the staging of a small greenhouse produce an effect of clean brilliance, which I suppose is enhanced by the light coming on all sides, and overhead, through glass; and also because each bloom is unsmirched by rain or soil-splash, unnibbled by slugs, and unpecked by birds. Furthermore, the grayness of the stone chippings with which you will, I hope, have sprinkled your pans, throws up the colors into

strong relief. Ideally, the pans should be whitewashed, for no one can pretend that the red of a flowerpot is pleasing, or of an agreeable texture.

Some of the little primulas lend themselves very happily to this treatment, *P. marginata*, for instance, or the lovely pale lavender Linda Pope; or even a clump of the ordinary blue primrose which suffers so from the mischief of birds when growing out of doors in the garden. I would like also to see a pan of larger size, interplanted with some of the choicer varieties of common bulbs, coming up between the primulas: the intensely blue hanging bells of *Scilla* Spring Beauty, or the pale blue of *Chionodoxa*, which resembles a tiny lily. Endless variations could be played on different color schemes; you could have a cool pan of yellow primroses interplanted with the white grape hyancinth and the white chionodoxa; or, for something looking rich and ecclesiastical, a pan of that very ordinary magenta *Primula juliana* Wanda with the inky blue *Muscari latifolium* amongst it. The gray cushions of saxifrage, with their miniature pink or rosy flowers, look charming in low pans with some stones to set them off, but these, I think, should be grown by themselves, not interplanted.

It is too late this year, of course, and is an idea to materialize twelve months hence. It may be a bit of a time-taker for busy people, but a welcome occupation for an invalid or a convalescent.

A race of little irises

THERE IS A RACE of little irises, flowering in spring, and too seldom grown. They do not aspire to make a great splash; their colors are frail; they grow only six to twelve inches high; they demand a small place to match their small size; they must be regarded as intimate flowers, to be peered into and protected from the vulgar slug. I am referring to miniature versions of the Bearded Iris, which is the sort most familiar to most people. These miniature versions are called *Iris pumila* and *I. chamaeiris*.

I will not waste space quarreling over botanical differences. I will say only that if you can buy what nurserymen usually term *Iris pumila* you will get a reward. There is *I. azurea*, and *I. coerulea*, and *I. lutea*, a yellow one. Having bought them, where is it best to plant them?

The authorities seem to differ in their opinion. W. R. Dykes, who was the great authority on irises, says that *Iris pumila* ought to be divided and transplanted every second year. He says they exhaust the soil. Yet I have grown a patch of them in a stone trough for some ten years and they have never flowered better than this year. The behavior of plants is indeed inexplicable. It breaks all the rules; and that is what makes gardening so endlessly various and interesting.

I have come to the conclusion, after many years of sometimes sad experience, that you cannot come to any conclusion at all. But one simple thing I have discovered in gardening; a simple thing one never sees mentioned in gardening books. It is the fact that many plants do better if they can get their roots under stones. This is a fact I would like to return to. In the meantime, since I set out to mention the little early irises, may I suggest that you might plant them into the cracks between paving or along the edges of a paved path, where they will not be walked on? I feel sure that this is the place to grow them, rather than down the front of a border, as is often recommended in books about gardening. They are not things for an herbaceous border: they are things for stone paths, surely; and the gray background of the paving enhances their delicacy of coloring. The worst that can be said against them is that they do not remain very long in flower, but they are so unobtrusive and take up so little room that their short flowering life entitles them to a place where they can subsequently grow forgotten.

An up-to-date aid to horticulture

INTEREST IS BEING increasingly taken in vermiculite, so although I don't know very much about it I think I should at least be fulfilling a duty in mentioning it. Such a nice clean thing to handle, beige in color, like the finest possible oatmeal, with little shiny bits of mica to brighten it up.

This up-to-date aid to horticulture is made of mica, an ore which is mined in the United States, in South Africa, in Uruguay, and Uganda.

Terrible things are done to it before it comes into our hands: it gets heated up to 2000 degrees Fahrenheit to make it expand; I hope not so painful a process as it sounds. Thus expanded or exfoliated, it becomes feather-weight and incredibly absorbent of moisture; in fact, from the driest oatmeal it will take on all the characteristics of a sponge that doesn't dry out.

Its primary use at present for the majority of amateurs is for propagation by means of cuttings, which are said to root in it more easily than in other forms of compost. It should first be thoroughly soaked in water, and then lightly and gently squeezed out, when it is unlikely that you will have to moisten it again before the cuttings have taken root. Do not leave them in the vermiculite longer than necessary, since it provides no nourishment for the little plants, but set them out to grow on in the soil or compost you would normally use. They may suffer a slight check after this transplanting, but that is nothing to worry about.

It can be used to fill seed boxes or pots, or to make up a bed in a frame, according to the quantity you are prepared to buy and the quantity of cuttings you wish to strike.

You should be careful to get a brand where the pH value is stated, as obviously too akaline or too acid a content would disagree with some cuttings. The neutral pH7 is best.

Vermiculite may be used many times over, thus making it more economical than might appear at first sight.

It must be understood that vermiculite is still at an experimental stage, though it has been known to advanced horticulturists for several years. Considerable possibilities are claimed for it in the improvement and aeration of soils, especially lawns; in the cultivation of tomatoes and mushrooms; in the raising of lilies from seed and scales; and for use in tubs and window boxes, owing to the extreme lightness compared with a filling of ordinary soil. Only, if you decide to try it for this purpose, you must supply nourishment in the form of liquid manure, remembering that vermiculite is merely a rooting medium and contains nothing of food value.

It is certainly worth a trial when the time for taking cuttings comes round. It would be interesting to set one batch in the sandy mixture you habitually use, and a similar batch in vermiculite, and watch the results.

Bearers of romantic names

THIS, I FEAR, is not going to be a very practical discussion. It will be of no use at all to anybody who is making or planting a garden. But as it is April Fools' Day I may perhaps be allowed a frivolity for once.

The frivolity concerns a nurseryman's catalog dated 1838. Queen Victoria had recently come to the throne. One of her humbler subjects, Mr. John Miller, of the Durdham Down Nursery, near Bristol, had just died as a bankrupt. His executors were carrying on his Business, for the benefit of the Creditors including the Bankrupt's immediate Relatives.

Poor Mr. John Miller. He had a magnificent list of plants for disposal, not only roses, but pelargoniums, auriculas, pinks, orchids, herbaceous plants—pages and pages of them. It seems a shame that he should go smash so soon after his young Queen had embarked on a reign of over sixty years of prosperity. He should have prospered with her; evidently he did not.

The reason why I here revive his list is not so much because I feel sorry for Mr. Miller, dead and lost 120 years ago, as because I think his catalog may interest rose specialists and may also appeal to those who share my appreciation for such names as these, picked at random:—

Monstrous four seasons; Belle sans flatterie; Black African; La belle Junon; Ninon de l'Enclos; Temple d'Apollon; Conque de Venus.

Where have they gone, these bearers of fantastically romantic names? If Edmond Rostand had known of them he would surely have put a great speech about them into the mouth of Cyrano de Bergerac. Where are they now? Lost, I suppose, for ever, unless they could be discovered in some ancient garden in England or France.

One of those queer quirks of memory that sometimes assail us made me take down from my shelves a copy of *The Rose Fancier's Manual,* translated from the French by Mrs. Gore, once a best-seller amongst novelists. I found, as I expected, that Mrs. Gore's book exactly corresponded in date, 1838, with the list of Mr. Miller, deceased. She mentions a number of the same roses, but she also mentions others which Mr. Miller had not got, or perhaps had sold out of. Her *Coupe d'amour* does not figure in Mr. Miller's list; nor does *Tout aimable;* nor does the rose whose name, if truthful, makes me want to possess it more than any: *Rien ne me surpasse.*

Surely the most exacting should be satisfied with that.

Daylilies are obliging plants

EASTER DAY, loveliest and youngest of feasts. I can hardly bring myself to think about summer, which to me always seems middle-aged compared with the adolescence of March, April, and even May. March is seventeen, though by no means always sweet; April is eighteen; May is nineteen; June is twenty to twenty-five; and then July leaps to thirty and thirty-five; and then August from forty to fifty; September to a mature, mellow sixty; October to an even mellower, yellower seventy; and then comes the leafless calm of the descending year.

Still, one must be practical, thinking of summer, if one is to fill up the gaps in one's garden, and I have been forcing myself to think about it in terms of the *Hemerocallis*, or daylily. This used to be regarded as a common old plant, almost a weed, when we grew the type which spread everywhere and was only a pale orange thing, not worth having. Now there are many fine hybrids, which may come as a revelation to those who have not yet seen them.

They will grow either in sun or shade. They will grow in damp soil, even by the waterside if you are so fortunate as to have a stream or a pond in your garden, when their trumpets of amber, apricot, orange, ruddle, and Venetian red will double themselves in reflection in the water. They will grow equally well in an ordinary bed or border. They are, in fact, extremely obliging plants, thriving almost anywhere.

They are especially useful for the summer garden, flowering as they do from July into September. Mostly in July and August.

A dignified and comely magnolia

THE GREAT WHITE *Magnolia denudata*, or yulan tree, began to open its flowers along its leafless branches on Easter Saturday, a magnificent sight against the pale blue of the April sky. The cool weather we endured throughout February and March this year suited its arrangements perfectly, for a warm spell during the early months tends to hurry it up, and then the flowers are liable to damage by their two enemies, frost and wind. I wonder that this most lovely of flowering trees is not more often planted. It is of reasonably rapid growth, eventually attaining a height of between twenty and forty feet, and, unlike some of the other magnolias such as *M. Kobus*, has the merit of flowering when still quite young. Any good garden loam suits it, especially if some decayed leaf mold can be added. It is best planted in April or May, and the vital thing to remember is that it must never be allowed to suffer from drought before it has become established. Once firmly settled into its new home, it can be left to look after itself. Avoid planting it in a frost pocket, or in a position where it will be exposed to the rays of a warm sun after a frosty night: under the lee of a north or west wall is probably the ideal situation, or within the shelter of a shrubbery.

This dignified and comely tree has been known in our gardens since 1789, when it was introduced from China by one of the collectors financed by that enlightened patron of plant hunters, Sir Joseph Banks. In China it had been known for far longer than that; in fact, for some 1300 years, growing beside temples and in the garden of the Summer Palace. Presumably it gets caught by frost in its native home also; frost spells ruin to the year's crop of flowers, and people who for reasons of limited space feel unwilling to take the risk, in spite of the immense reward in a favorable season, would be better advised to plant the later-flowering *Magnolia soulangeana,* less pure in its whiteness, for the outside of the petals is stained with pink or purple; or *Magnolia lennei,* which is frankly rosy, but very beautiful with its huge pink goblets, and seldom suffers from frost unless it has extremely bad luck at the end of April or when those three mischievous ice-saints hold their festival in the middle of May.

A hint from nature

MAY I GO BACK to something I wrote a while ago about many plants doing so well if they can get their roots under stones? I am not thinking specially of Alpines whose natural habit it is, but of casual strays, often self-sown, sometimes bulbous plants, sometimes merely annuals or biennials, which by a successful accident have pointed the way to this method of gardening. The narrowest crack in a path or paved terrace will surprisingly send up the finest seedling; I have known even such large unwanted subjects as delphiniums and hollyhocks to make the attempt. The reason, obviously, is that they never suffer from either excessive moisture or excessive drought; the stone preserves such moisture as is in the soil, but prevents the soggy puddling consequent on a heavy rainfall; furthermore, it protects from the scorching sun and consequent wilting which demands the watering can.

If we are to take this hint from nature it would be as well to dispose of the weeds first to save trouble later on. Weeds in paths are a constant worry to those who have not discovered the ghoulish pleasure of using weed-killer; and, even to the initiate, the cost of proprietary weed-killers is often a deterrent, driving many a conscientious gardener back to the kneeling-pad and the broken knife blade. It is now possible, however, to buy sodium chlorate by the pound; as you must use only one pound to ten gallons of water, it works out very cheaply. Sodium chlorate acts through the leaves, so should be applied when the weeds are green—the only drawback is that the ground is not safe to set other plants in for about six months. I should then fill up the cracks with good soil or compost, and sow quite recklessly. I should not mind how ordinary my candidates were, forget-me-not, pansies, wallflowers, Indian pinks, alyssum, because I should pull up 95 per cent later on, leaving only single specimens here and there. It is not, after all, a flower bed that we are trying to create. If, however, you think it is a waste of opportunity to sow such ordinary things, there are plenty of low-growing plants of a choicer kind, especially those which dislike excessive damp at the root throughout the winter: this covering of stone would protect them from that. The old-fashioned pinks would make charming tufts. *Dianthus allwoodii*, for example, with their suggestion of chintz and of patchwork quilts, should succeed under such conditions; I confess to repeated failures with them in open borders, but their neatness and variety encourage perseverance.

Growing Alpines in tubs

GROWING STRAWBERRIES in tubs or barrels is a good idea for people who have a limited area of garden. You waste no ground space, and you set your tubs anywhere you want them, either side of the front door or sideways along the garden path. It now occurs to me that the idea could be extended to Alpines or other small plants, growing in the same way in barrels sawn in half round their equator.

Why not? It is an easy idea to carry out. You buy your barrel from a local sale; put a thick layer of crocks all over the bottom, not forgetting to pierce a hole or holes for drainage first; you then fill it with soil and plant your treasures. The kind of soil you fill it with will depend upon what kind of treasures you wish to grow. Alpines, generally speaking, like a somewhat gritty soil which will afford them the good, open drainage that prevents them from rotting off. A gritty soil may be achieved by mixing a barrowful of fibrous loam, taken from the top-spit of an old meadow, with some sharp sand and a generous helping of stone chippings such as one sees piled in such enticing heaps by the roadside.

Flat-growing subjects such as saxifrages would probably be best for a groundwork on top, making squabs of silvery gray, something like a round Victorian pincushion, breaking out into their tiny rosy flowers in the spring. The sorts called *Saxifraga irvingii, jenkinsonii,* and Cranbourne are all very small, tight, and pretty. But you can be more ambitious with your barrel if you want to plant other things half way up it. You can plant things which like pouring out sideways, making miniature waterfalls of flower, little Niagaras of foam in the saxifrage called Tumbling Waters—twelve inches long in its flower tassel, hanging down, very handsome and yet very delicate. Another plant I would like to set into the sideway holes of the sawn barrel is lewisia. The lewisias are not too easygoing, which is perhaps the reason they are so seldom seen; but they are certainly plants for any gardener prepared to accept a challenge. They make rosettes of leaf, and throw out sprays of chintz-like flowers, pink or creamy, very elegant and old-fashioned looking. They should do well planted sideways in the barrel, on the principle that they are very happy growing out of a dry wall; it should be remembered, however, that they dislike lime. They also dislike disturbance, and the best way to propagate them is by seed.

A serialized grape vine

WHY NOT EMULATE the ancient custom of making a hedge of grape vines? To do this, you allow your young vine to develop only one single rod, which you train horizontally, along a wire or along bamboo canes if you prefer, nailed to pegs driven into the soil; and when this rod has reached a length of thirteen feet, you bend the end of it downwards and push it firmly to a depth of six inches or more into the ground. It will then take root (we hope), and will spring up quite soon in new growth for the next rod, when you repeat the process over and over again, until your original vine with its recurrent progeny has attained the length you require.

You see the advantages. First, you need only one rootstock to start the process; very economical. (Of course, if you like to plant two, one at either end, it would go quicker, and they would meet in the middle, like engineers working through an Alpine tunnel.) Secondly, you can control your rods into any shape to suit the layout of your garden; you could grow them in a straight line down a long path, for example, or you could make them turn sharp corners at right angles to form an enclosure, vines being very flexible and tractable. Thirdly, by the time the rods have made old wood they should need no propping or staking; they will have grown tough enough to support themselves. Fourthly, you can, if you wish, grow this serialized vine a mile long. What a thought! Fifthly, you can eat the grapes.

The foam of spiraea

ONE OF THE PRETTIEST and easiest of spring-flowering shrubs is surely *Spiraea arguta*, more descriptively known as bridal wreath or foam of May. In a warm season it may well start foaming in April; and foam it does, for every one of its black twiggy growths is smothered tight with innumerable tiny white flowers. In fact you cannot see the plant for the flowers.

It likes a sunny place; is happy in any decent loam; does not object to a slightly calcareous soil; makes a rounded bush about six feet high; and can be increased by layering. There is an earlier one called *Spiraea thunbergii*, whose leaves are said to color well in autumn.

Obviously the pure candor of its whiteness would look

best against the dark background of a yew hedge, or any dark shrubs if yew is not available. There comes a moment at twilight when white plants gleam with a peculiar pallor or ghostliness. I dare to say of white, that neutral tint usually regarded as an *absence* of color, that it is every bit as receptive of changing light as the blues and reds and purples. It may perhaps demand a patiently observing eye, attuned to a subtlety less crude than the strong range of reds and purples that we get in, say, the herbaceous phloxes which miraculously alter their hue as the evening light sinks across them. I love color, and rejoice in it, but white is lovely to me forever. The ice-green shades that it can take on in certain lights, by twilight or by moonlight, perhaps by moonlight especially, make a dream of the garden, an unreal vision, yet one knows that it isn't unreal at all because one has planted it all for effect.

An Alpine meadow

ONCE, YEARS AGO, I wrote about a thyme lawn I had made, a simple and rather obvious idea which met with a surprising response in popularity, but I don't think I have ever written about an Alpine lawn. Those fortunate people who have walked over the high Alpine pastures of Switzerland or French Savoy or the Austrian Dolomites will know what I mean. In that clean, pure air, fresh as iced water and fluty as a glass of hock, the bright flowers bejewel the turf and cluster up against the natural out-

crops of gray rock, edging the quick, narrow rills, silvery
as minnows as they trickle from their source: blowing in
the mountain breeze and crouching inch-low to the
ground in an instinct of self-protection against the mountain gales.

We cannot aspire to so majestic a setting, but in a humble way we can reproduce a patch of Alpine meadow in
our own gardens. It makes the ideal approach to the little
foothills of a rock garden. The essential thing is to make
it as dense as possible; it must be woven tight as a carpet
or a tapestry. Clearly, we cannot use grass as a foundation,
unless we are prepared to clip it with nail scissors, so I
suggest some of the close-carpeting plants: the creeping
thymes, the little mints, the common yellow stonecrop,
the camomile, the blue veronica, anything which crawls
and creeps and mats itself into a green drugget mosaiced
in its season by its small gay flowers. If the spring-flowering *Gentiana acaulis* will grow for you, so much the better;
it usually grows all right, forming a thick green mat, even
if it does not flower, and a thick green mat is all-important.
I should not mind some aubretia, discreetly used and not
allowed to encroach, nor should I mind some wild violets.

The question of moisture is almost bound to arise. Such
an underground mesh of little greedy roots will suck every
drop from the ground. In the real Alpine meadow there
are many small springs, the ground may even be quite
spongy, where you may find such things as the magenta
Saxifraga oppositifolia, but such blessings are rare. A good
substitute for the natural spring or streamlet is a form
of hose known as the snake-irrigator. As its name implies,

it can be made to wriggle wherever wanted, and as it is
made of porous canvas it oozes gently, damping the area
without any waste of water. I have only just acquired this,
and am greatly taken with it, as, unlike some gadgets, it
seems to do exactly what it claims to do.

Clematis are almost perfect climbers

HOWEVER POPULAR, however ubiquitous, the clematis must remain among the best hardy climbers in our
gardens. Consider first their beauty, which may be either
flamboyant or delicate. Consider their long flowering
period, from early spring until frost. Consider also that
they are easy to grow; appreciate lime in the soil; are
readily propagated, especially by layering; are very attractive even when not in flower, with their silky-silvery
seedheads, which always remind me of Yorkshire terriers
curled into a ball; offer an immense variety both of species
and hybrids; and may be used in many different ways,
for growing over sheds, fences, pergolas, hedges, old
trees, or up the walls of houses. The perfect climber?
Almost, but there are two snags which worry most people.
    There is the problem of pruning. This, I admit, is
complicated if you want to go into details, but as a rough
working rule it is safe to say that those kinds which flower
in the spring and early summer need pruning just after
they have flowered, whereas the later flowering kinds

(i.e., those that flower on the shoots they have made during the current season) should be pruned in the early spring.

The second worry is stem rot. You may prefer to call it *Ascochyta Clematidina*, but the result is the same, that your most promising plant will suddenly, without the slightest warning, be discovered hanging like miserable wet string. The cause is known to be a fungus, but the cure, which would be more useful to know, is unknown. The only comfort is that the plant will probably shoot up again from the root; you should, of course, cut the collapsed strands down to the ground to prevent any spread of the disease. It is important, also, to obtain plants on their own roots, for they are far less liable to attack.

Slugs, caterpillars, mice, and rabbits are all fond of young clematis, but that is just one of the normal troubles of gardening. Stem rot is the real specialty of the clematis.

There is much more to be said about this beautiful plant but space only to say that it likes shade at its roots, and don't let it get too dry.

Moral tangles

THERE IS NOTHING like the gentle, removing touch of slight illness to induce meditation over some experience recently enjoyed. One must not be *too* ill, only just ill enough to justify a couple of days in bed, with sufficient fever to heighten the perceptions. Life is laid aside; one is vaguely aware of a wood pigeon cooing in the distance; the tap of a thrush on a snail; the rustle of the breeze through poplars; all things very small but significant. In these moments, these brief dedicated hours with leisure enforced, one may ruminate as vacantly as a cow recumbent in her meadow.

In such a mood, I remembered going down into the wood to dig up some roots of a specially deep pink anemone. I had observed it growing there, and I knew from previous experience that if you are so fortunate as to discover a colored anemone occurring amongst the white ones, you can transplant it with every hope that it will come up again in the same color in your own garden. Vandals ignorantly dig up wild plants, at the wrong time, and treat them in such a way that they can never be expected to survive. I knew that I was doing right by my pink windflower in transplanting it to my garden. There was so much of it that it could well afford me a trowelful of its roots.

That trowelful of woodland soil taught me a lesson. It was so tightly crammed with growing things, all struggling for existence. Only a trowel, to disturb four square inches of ground in an English wood! There was a potential oak tree, sprouting from an acorn. There were young brambles, already in their innocence threatening invasion. There were young honeysuckles, inch high, preparing to hoist themselves towards the light with the twiggy support of the hazel coppice. All a living tangle underground, struggling together, and me the superior human with my sharp weapon, prising up the chosen plant

I wanted, destroying all that other scrambling and wrestling life, which might have come to completion had I not interfered.

Lying feverish in my bed I wondered whether I had done wrong or right. A whole crop of moral tangles came up. I had frustrated a young oak. But I had preserved a pink windflower. Where was the answer to be found in virtue?

Not in the least reptilian

SOME TIME AGO I mentioned a new gadget I had discovered, called the snake-irrigator. As a rule I mistrust new gadgets because the old trusty servants usually turn out to do their jobs far better, centuries of experience having gone to their making. When all is done and tried out, nothing will hammer in a nail better than a hammer, not even the heel of a shoe, or dig better than a spade, or rake better than a rake, or hoe better than a hoe.

All the same this snake-irrigator promises to be a real addition to the armory of the toolshed. Someone suggested that it was an inauspicious name, owing to its unfortunate association with the Garden of Eden, but do not allow that to deter you. It is not in the least reptilian, being made of nice clean white canvas; and, unlike snakes, it is wet, not dry. The brittle dryness of snakes is the thing that puts some people against them, quite apart from the atavistic though reasonable fear of getting bitten. The snake-irrigator has neither the wish nor the ability to bite. The only thing it has in common with snakes or serpents is its ability to wriggle. It will wriggle in any direction, but at your own desire, not its. This is obviously its supreme advantage. You can make it go wherever you need it. You attach it either to a tap within the house, or to a length of ordinary garden hose, and then you leave it to ooze and seep and soak all through the night or day without any further trouble to yourself. You just leave it on and turn the tap off when it has done its job; but, having now tried it in practice, I made one discovery: it does not like kinks. It likes either a straight run, or else wide sweeps and circles.

One can imagine many uses for it: round newly planted trees or shrubs; on a bed of seeds or seedlings; to create an artificial swamp for moisture-loving plants, such as some primulas; to encourage the spring growth of amaryllis or some lilies, to save drooping plants from drought in summer.

It occurs to me to wonder what the water company would have to say to it, though it is most economical of water and there is no wastage. We are fortunate where I live in having a deep old rain-reservoir piped to the garden, with the only disadvantage that a little eft sometimes gets stuck in the pipe. Failing this endless and independent supply, siphonage from a rain-water butt or a pond might be the solution, when one of these threatening notices arrives, forbidding the use of water for garden or garage.

Very small gardens

FROM TIME TO TIME I get letters from owners of very small gardens, asking what to do about them. These letters usually come from truly keen amateur gardeners, otherwise they would not take the trouble to write. May I quote from a typical letter? "Our plot is the usual commonplace rectangle, 45 ft. by 175 ft., but I am resolved *not* to have a commonplace garden. Our house stands 40 ft. back from the road, with this pocket-handkerchief frontage. . . . We hope to plant a camomile lawn, and I have ideas about a lavender hedge . . . and we want one or two trees, *not* the usual suburban pink cherry. . . ."

Now this is evidently a gardener after my own heart; and there must be many of them up and down the country. They are restricted as to space, but not restricted in their imaginative ideas. Why, indeed, should anyone have a commonplace garden in the commonplace rectangle? Endless variations are possible, and endless suggestions could be made. For my own part, if I were suddenly required to leave my own garden and to move into a bungalow in a housing development, I should have no hesitation at all about ruffling the front garden into a wildly unsymmetrical mess and making it as near as possible into a cottage garden, which is probably the prettiest form of gardening ever achieved in this country in its small and unambitious way. I should plant only the best things in it, and only the best forms of the best things, by which I mean that everything should be choice and chosen. When you have only a very small area to your command you cannot afford to be otherwise than selective. Thus, if I had a lawn, it should be of the purest turf; and if I had shrubs they should be specially picked out, the very best lilacs, for example; and if I had bulbs for spring

flowering, they should be of the loveliest, most delicate sorts, coming up through clumps of violets smothering the ground; bulbs of scilla and chionodoxa and the grape hyacinth and the dogtooth violet, and some fritillaries, but always the best and most unusual forms of these; and if I had annuals and biennials to fill up the gaps, they should always be the best, whether they were pansies or carnations.

Naturally, every garden must be a law to itself. So much

depends upon soil, aspect, and the taste of the owner. More depends upon his taste than upon his purse. A comforting reflection to end up on.

Amiable and floriferous shrubs

THERE ARE TWO very pretty spring flowering shrubs not difficult to grow but for some reason not very commonly seen. They go well together, both being of the same shade of a delicate shell pink and both belonging to the same botanical family (*caprifoliaceae*), which includes the more familiar weigelias and the honeysuckles, with small trumpet-shaped flowers dangling from graceful sprays. These two shrubs are *Kolkwitzia amabilis* and *Dipelta floribunda*.

Kolkwitzia, appropriately called beauty bush, comes into flower a little later than the dipelta, and thus provides a useful succession in the same coloring; in other words, a combination of the two would ensure a cloud of pale pink over a considerable number of weeks. It ought to be planted in front of the dipelta, as it tends to make a more rounded bush, whereas the dipelta grows taller and looser, and flops enough to require a few tall stakes. Both come from China, and each deserves the other's adjective, as well as its own, for they are both amiable and floriferous.

While on the subject of spring flowering shrubs, I might mention *Rubus deliciosus*. This comes from the

Rocky Mountains, and is a bramble, but not thorny. I cannot imagine why this lovely and easygoing thing should be so foolishly neglected. If you are acquainted with the big, single white rose Nevada, you will readily make a mental picture of *Rubus deliciosus*, for I notice that people usually mistake it for the rose until, on looking closer, they become surprised to find it blowing among leaves like the leaves of a blackcurrant. It will reach eight feet and more in height, great arching sprays which may require a few bamboo canes for a light support. Apart from this it involves no labor, except an occasional cutting-out of dead wood.

This is a *Rubus* for spring, but it has a Himalayan relation in *Rubus biflorus*, the white-washed bramble, which is grown less for the sake of its insignificant flowers than for the beauty of its pure white stems in winter. Tall ghosts, they make a surprising apparition in the winter landscape, suggesting a plant permanently coated with rime. It likes a rich soil, and a gentle climate, and you have to cut down the stems which have flowered, and probably fruited, the previous year because the young growth is what you need to encourage and retain.

Water is the making of a garden

IT SOMETIMES HAPPENS that people inherit, or acquire, an old dwelling house or cottage with a pool or even with the remains of a moat. Presumably, such surroundings are highly picturesque, and the fortunate owner wants to make the most of them. Let us assume also that no previous owner has bothered about suitable planting, and has left the waterside to ramp away into a terrible mess of unworthy weeds.

Water is the making of a garden. It gives a rare chance to the gardener. He can grow things *in* the water, and *beside* the water, and even *on* the water—a triple pleasure, far more agreeable than the filling up of triplicate forms. I will take *in* and *on* the water first.

Waterlilies come first to the mind; and apart from the white and yellow ones, there are hybrids in pink, red, and primrose. Twelve to eighteen inches of water-depth is a safe rough guide, and full sun. The usual method is to sink the plants in an old basket, when they will root through the basket into the bottom mud; but they can also be tied between two turfs and sunk (the right way up). Late May or early June is the time. If you think the leaves of waterlilies too large for a small pond, there is the bog bean with small white flowers, floating; or *Pontederia cordata*, like a pale blue arum. For the edges, where the water is not so deep, our yellow flag iris is both lovely and reliable; the flowering rush, *Butomus umbellatus*, is an arrowy grower three to four feet high with rosy flowers; it looks exotic, but is in fact to be found wild in Britain. *Sagittaria*, the true arrowhead, white flowers, associates well with this rather spiky group.

For something lower in stature on the boggy margin, the water forget-me-not, *Myosotis palustris*, is a great spreader of a china blue, paler than the garden varieties.

The king cup or marsh marigold will grow either in sun or shade, which is obliging of it.

Finally, the very brave could experiment with the ordinary white arum, the lily of the Nile, which, if planted deep enough, should survive an average winter in the south. But if you want to grow arums out of doors in water, the bog arum, *Calla palustris,* is a less risky investment.

In choosing plants for the waterside, I think it is important to remember that their beauty will be doubled if you can arrange for them to be reflected in the water. If the water is covered by floating plants, such as water-lilies, this will not be possible, though one can usually contrive to keep a bare zone round the outside to serve as a mirror. Much will depend, of course, on whether the pond has banked-up sides, or fades away into a swampy level; these are differences which can only be considered on the spot.

For the marshy swamp I would suggest a drift of the moisture-loving primulas: *P. japonica, chionantha, bulleyana, helodoxa,* known as the glory of the marsh. If economy is a consideration, as it usually is, these primulas are all easily raised from seed. The tall clematis-like Japanese irises, *I. kaempferi,* look most beautiful growing amongst them, but I always think their requirements are a little awkward to manage—wet in summer, dry in winter. Nature's water supply usually works the other way around. The blue *Iris laevigata,* on the other hand, does not mind boggy conditions all the year through. *Iris sibirica,* less large and handsome than the Japanese, is exceedingly graceful and pretty and most accommodating, though it does not like being too deeply drowned. *Iris delvayi* resembles it, and is useful because it flowers later, when *sibirica* is over. The richer the soil, the better for all these irises, even to a mulch of rotted manure. These are all tall-growing, but if you can spare a special corner, marking it off with a ring of rough stones, do try the little almost-black gold-veined *I. chrysographes*, a real gem; and *I. fulva*, a coppery red.

So much for the waterside irises, but coming higher up on the bank, assuming that there is a bank, and that it is dry, I think one might plant the scarlet dogwood, *Cornus alba*. Do not be misled by the name; *alba* in this case refers only to the flowers, which are silly, contemptible little things in summer. The glory of this plant is the red bark of its bare stems throughout the winter. Caught by the light of the sinking sun, reflected in water, it is as warming to the heart as a log-fire on the hearth after a cold day.

For the bamboo-minded

A GENTLEMAN WRITES to complain that he cannot find anyone bamboo-minded and will I please tell him how and when to break up and transplant a clump he has found growing in his garden.

I cannot claim, and indeed would not wish to claim, to be bamboo-minded. I hate the horrid Victorian-looking things nearly as much as I hate pampas grass. But I could at any rate inform my correspondent that if he insisted on shifting his bamboos from one part of his garden to another, the spring was the right time to do it, and I could also advise him to keep the divided roots heavily watered until they had settled down in their new place.

I wish him joy of them, and am grateful to him for his letter, since it sent me to a consideration of this plant with the queerest peculiarities. It looks so drab and dingy in our gardens, but if you think of its uses in other lands you may come to entertain a kindly regard for it. You may use it as a torch to light your way through the jungle. You may eat it, pickle it, and make practically anything out of it, from a dwelling-house to a gramophone needle. It will make a mast for your boat, furniture for your room, fences for your encampment, and paper for your correspondence. This alarming grass, moreover, must look truly impressive when it grows sixteen inches in one day and reaches a height of over a hundred feet. But perhaps the oddest thing about it is its inexplicable habit of flowering at intervals of roughly thirty years, when every growth of a certain species blooms simultaneously over widely separated areas, with the ensuing death of the plant, a mystery of nature which suggests an analogy with the seasonal stirring of some wines, even though they may have been transported from their native land to the antipodes.

Scented flowers

I HAVE BEEN ASKED to write about scented flowers in the garden and in the greenhouse. What a delightful subject, and why did I never think of it for myself? So often I wonder what to write about, and here comes a heaven-sent suggestion.

I must take the garden first, and leave the greenhouse till later on. We all have gardens, but we don't all have greenhouses. The first thing to say about scents in the open is that there are relatively few plants whose scent will hang on the air in such a way as to make you sniff in inquiry as you walk past. Many things smell good when you push your nose into them, or crush them, or bring them into a warm room, but what we are thinking about is the garden path as we stroll, something that will really hit you in surprise. I think my choice would be:

An edging of Cheddar pinks.
A hedge of hybrid Musk roses, especially Penelope.
Some bushes of the rugosa rose, *Blanc double de coubert*.
Azaleas.
A hedge of sweetbrier.
The balsam poplar when it first unfolds its sticky leaves.
Lilium auratum, as a luxury.

I know everyone will disagree and everyone will have other ideas of his own. I quite expect a spate of suggestions about the things I have left out, for in the region of the five senses the sense of smell (and the allied sense of taste) is highly controversial. Some people love the scent of phlox; to me, it suggests pigsties, not that I dislike pigsties, being country-born, and well accustomed to them. Much depends also on the keenness of the nose, and also on the fact that not all scented plants give off their scent all the time. They may vary with the temperature, with the degree of moisture in the air, and even with the time of day. This capriciousness makes them perhaps more precious. One may catch an unexpected whiff as one passes a bush of wintersweet or witch-hazel, not to be detected an hour ago. And the scent of box in the sun, and of box clippings as you crush them underfoot. And of a bed of warm wallflowers. And the night-scented stock, that lackluster annual which comes into its own after twilight.

But perhaps there is nothing to equal the woodland acres of our native bluebell, *Scilla nonscripta*, smoke blue as an autumn bonfire, heavy in scent as a summer rose, yet young as the spring which is its season.

Some flowering currants

THE OLD FLOWERING currant, *Ribes sanguineum*, is a familiar sight in cottage gardens, where it may sometimes be seen clipped into shape as a hedge, and a very dense, pretty hedge it makes, clothed at this time of year with a mass of pink flowers. A most reliable shrub, never taking a year off, and demanding the minimum of care or cultivation, it cannot lay claim to great distinction, and indeed some people despise the somewhat dingy pink of the individual flower; these people, with whom I find myself in agreement, should not be satisfied with the original type, introduced from the west of the United States in 1826, but should obtain its varieties Splendens and King Edward VII, both far brighter in color and just as accommodating in temperament.

I suppose that most people know the tip of cutting generous sheaves of the common flowering currant in late winter and putting them in a pail of water indoors, where they will come into flower purely white.

There are, however, other *Ribes* less often seen. One of these is *Ribes speciosum*, which I can liken only to a prickly fuchsia. As cross and spiny as a gooseberry, this Californian dangles annually during spring with quantities of miniature red fuchsia-like flowers, hung in rows of little tassels all along its reddish young shoots. If trained against a wall these shoots will stick out horizontally to a length of twelve or eighteen inches with very charming effect, especially if the shrub can be planted where the sunlight will strike the shoots, turning them almost to the blood-red transparency of a garnet or of a dog's pricking ear, backed by a bright light. Except in cold districts, it will grow quite happily as a bush in the open; but there is no doubt that it does make a very decorative wall-covering and you will find that it considerably puzzles people who have never seen it before.

There is also *Ribes aureum*, which I find described in an old catalog as the buffalo currant of the Wild West. The flowers, in this case, are yellow; and have the advantage, for those who like cloves, of diffusing that spicy scent, and there is the further advantage that the leaves in autumn will turn to a fine gold.

Killing slugs humanely

THERE IS A FORM of hypocrisy common to nearly all gardeners. It does not affect only the gentle amateurs, but has been known to affect even the most hardened professional, who is not, generally speaking, a sentimental or squeamish man. It is the human weakness which, accompanying our determination to rid ourselves of our slugs and snails, makes us reluctant next morning to contemplate the result of our over-night efforts.

Having enjoyed our own good breakfast, we come out to behold the slimy greenish remains. Big black slugs, four inches long; little black slugs, one inch long; snails exuding their entrails from under their beautiful delicate shells. . . . Poison has done its work only too well. In what agony, during the dark hours, have these miserable members of God's Creation perished? We ordained it, knowing, nay, hoping for what would happen; but when we see it we do not like it. We remember the lyrical terms in which the poets have addressed our victims:

> *To note on hedgerow baulks, in moisture sprent,*
> *The jetty snail creep from the mossy thorn,*

With earnest heed, and tremulous intent,
Frail brother of the morn!

Shakespeare also had a flattering comparison for him:

Love's feeling is more soft and sensible
Than are the tender horns of cockled snails.

It is all very painful, unpleasant, and even nauseating. What is to be done about it? We must abolish our frail brother with his tender horns, or else sacrifice our seedlings: we have the choice. The seedlings, I think, will win; must win. We must kill their enemies, but, if we are humane in our hearts, we will commit this slaughter with the least distressing offense to our hypocritical selves.

I think I have found the answer in an anti-slug bait which causes slugs and snails to shrivel up, dryly. It is Snarol; and it really works. It is said to be harmless to plants, birds, and animals. And all I hope is that it doesn't cause unnecessary suffering to those humble enemies who creep across our paths, and have to be destroyed.

Risk an acacia in a warm corner

MANY YEARS AGO, in the high mountains of Persia, I collected some seed pods off a mimosa which was most unaccountably growing there, some 5000 feet above sea level, and some hundred miles from any spot whence it could possibly be considered as a garden escape. I do not pretend to explain how it came there, in that cold, stony, snowy, desolate region; all I know is that there it was, and that I brought seeds home, and now have a tree of it growing out of doors in my garden and a vase full of it on my table, smelling not of the snows but of the warm south.

I think it is probably *Acacia dealbata* and not a true mimosa at all, but it looks so like what we call mimosa in the florists' shops or on the French Riviera that the name may conveniently serve. Botanists may write to tell me that it is more likely to be *Albizzia julibrissin*, a native of Persia, whereas the acacia is a native of Australia, which adds to the mystery of how it came to be growing on the Elburz mountains; but *Albizzia* it certainly is not.

All this preamble is intended to suggest that enterprising gardeners in the south might well risk a plant in a sheltered corner. Of course the ideal place is a large conservatory, but few people have large conservatories nowadays. It might not come unscathed through a terrible winter, but my tree at any rate has not so far turned a hair in frost, and the place where I found it growing was certainly more bleak and windswept than anything we can provide here. We take the precaution of wrapping its trunk and lower branches in trousers of sacking, and that is all the protection it gets. For greater safety, it could be trained fan-wise against a wall, if you started the training young enough. I should perhaps add that a high wall shelters it from the north, and that it is planted facing full south. I should add also that it is no good picking it before the flowers are fully out, in the hope that they will open in water; there are some things which refuse to oblige in that way, and this is one of them. You must wait till the clusters are as fluffy and yellow as ducklings.

It makes a charming pot plant until it becomes too large and has to be transferred into a tub or else planted out into the open ground.

The habit of pot gardening

THE HAPPY FEW who maintain a greenhouse, however small, sufficiently warmed in winter to keep the frost out, will find themselves repaid if they can make room for a few pots of the unfamiliar, pretty, blue-flowered *Oxypetalum caeruleum.** This, admittedly, is subtle rather than showy, but I notice that it always attracts attention when we stand the pots out of doors for the summer in the garden. It has downy-green leaves and flowers of a curious grayish blue, with a bright blue button no bigger than a flattened seed-pearl in the middle. I like to associate it with some pots of *Plumbago capensis*, whose stronger blue marries into a mist of blues reinforcing one another. Both, of course, are cool greenhouse plants, but they will live very happily in the open from the end of May until October.

I like the habit of pot gardening. It reminds me of the south—Italy, Spain, Provence, where pots of carnations

* *Oxypetalum caeruleum* is now known as *Tweedia caerulea*, or *Amblyopetalum caeruleum*. It is a native of Brazil.

and zinnias are stood carelessly about, in a sunny courtyard or rising in tiers on the treads of an outside stair,
dusty but oh how gay! I know it entails constant watering,
but consider the convenience of being able to set down
a smear of color just where you need it, in some corner
where an earlier flower has gone off. We should take this
hint from other lands. We do not make nearly enough
use of pots in our country, partly, I suspect, because we
have no tradition of pot-making here, nothing to compare
with the camellia pot, a common thing in Italy, swagged
with garlands looped from a lion's mouth. Several times
have I tried to persuade brickmakers to reproduce this
standardized Italian model. They look at it with suspicion
and alarm. "Oh, no, we couldn't do that. We have never
done anything like that. Sorry, we can't oblige."

Meanwhile we surround a huge black Chinese jar with
the blue *Oxypetalum* and the blue plumbago all through
the summer, and drop a potful of morning glory,
Heavenly Blue, into the Chinese jar, to pour downwards
into a symphony of different blues.

The Chinese jar is of romantic origin. It was made during the Ming dynasty—which might mean anything between 1368 and 1644—and was used to transport porcelain
from China to Egypt, packed in lard to keep it from rat-
tling about. The very solid handles show where the ropes
were passed through, to sling it on board ship. It is not
really black, but a sort of aubergine color.

The secret of anemones

SO MANY PEOPLE have recently remarked to me, "We cannot get anemones to do, whereas with you they seem to grow like weeds," that I began to wonder what the explanation could be, and have come to the conclusion that they do not get planted at the right time. In other words, the little black tuber of the anemone hates being kept out of the ground for longer than need be. It sometimes may linger in a paper bag until you have time to plant it, and, furthermore, goodness knows how long it has been on its way between the nurseryman's garden and yours. Like impatient persons, it is annoyed by being kept waiting, but unlike impatient persons it takes a suitable revenge by merely withering and dying. How distressing it would be if such were the reaction of our friends and acquaintances whenever we were late for an appointment!

There are many different kinds of anemone, all very desirable in the spring garden, and I feel sure that the same rule applies to all: plant them as soon as their leaves have begun to die down and turn yellow. This is easy enough if you already have them in your garden and wish to divide them, or to replant, or to transfer them to a different site. It is not so easy if you are ordering them for the first time from a nurseryman, as you may then not be able to get them lifted fresh and plump in June, but may have to wait for what is called autumn delivery.

How bright and full of color they are, some of these anemones. *A. blanda*, the pale blue Greek, who flowers a fortnight earlier than *appenina*, the darker blue Italian; and then the successive crop of the scarlet *fulgens*, the delicate mauve *allenii*, and the paler mauve *robinsoniana*, all of them related to the windflower, the flower of Adonis, the flower of resurrection, the flower of spring. They have gone by now, and their leaves are dying away. This is the time to move them; I feel sure that is true of the anemones, as it is true of some other tuberous plants such as the winter aconite, which does not easily settle down unless you catch its seedlings and shift them with a lump of soil to their new place.

They must never be allowed to dry off. They must be jumped quick from one place into another. That is the moral of this tale.

A selective and intelligent weed-killer

THE WEEDS in the lawn are all curly. Dandelions, plantains, and the daisy leaves have all turned upwards as though they were raising small hands to heaven in one last despairing prayer. In a few weeks' time I hope, heartlessly, that they will have disappeared and their place be taken by a nice clean sward of irreproachable turf, so mistakenly supposed by overseas visitors to demand four centuries in the making.

They have been treated with Weedone weed-killer. It seems a miracle to me that any mere liquid out of a tin should be so selective and intelligent as to know what forms of vegetation it is intended to destroy, and what forms to spare; but such is the truth. I understand that what in fact happens is that the liquid stimulates the growth of the weeds to such an extent that the cells eventually burst themselves with excessive exuberance and the plant perishes, whereas the blades of grass remain unaffected. Very strange and manifold are the labor-saving devices which science now provides for the overworked gardener.

Instead of crawling about on all fours in solitary bad temper and incipient lumbago with a trowel or a broken kitchen knife, you may now promenade in a leisurely way, saunter up and down, sprinkling selective death from a watering can as you converse with the friends who have come to tea. Thus you combine social life with the gardening job you have not yet had time to do. Your friends may find you a bit absent minded, but you can always impress them into service if you have a spare watering can. Grown-ups, as well as children, like to feel that they are being useful: it gives a sense of importance.

The instructions sent with each tin are so clear that I have no need to repeat them here. I need remark only on the economy of the method. A small investment will cover many square yards of lawn. Plantains and the creeping buttercup respond quickly to this cruel but clever treatment; daisies and dandelions may require a second dose. And do not be discouraged if you see no real result for a month to two months. It works in the end.

But oh, how passionately I hope that selective weedkillers will never be used on the grass verges of our lanes. No weed-killer could be selective enough to spare the wild violets, the primroses, and Queen Anne's lace.

It is all a question of shape

I SHOULD LIKE to write here on a subject of general gardening interest. These remarks will inevitably apply to the larger type of garden where plants can be grown in generous masses, but I think and hope that they may also be applicable to the small garden as a matter of principle.

You see, I believe that one ought always to regard a garden in terms of architecture as well as of color. One has huge lumps of, let us say, the shrub roses making large voluminous bushes like a Victorian crinoline, or flinging themselves about in wild sprays; or, putting it another way, some plants make round fat bushes, and seem to demand a contrast in a tall sharp plant, say delphiniums, sticking up in a cathedral spire of bright blue amongst the roses instead of in the orthodox way at the back of a herbaceous border. It is all a question of shape. Architectural shape, demanding the pointed thin ones amongst the fat rounds, as a minaret rises above the dome of a mosque.

Let me say here, for the small garden, that one might happily cause some spikes of the pink *Linaria* Canon J. Went to rise above a carpeting of low pansies or violas. This linaria comes true from seed; sows itself everywhere like a welcome, not an unwelcome, weed; and is as pretty a thing as you could wish to have in quantities for picking for the house indoors.

Another fine thing to make great steeples is yucca. This will tower in a vast heavy ivory pyramid in July, of a powerful architectural value. It does not flower every year, so you must have at least three plants in order to get a yearly blooming, and for this you need a certain amount of space. I did begin by saying that this would be addressed to people with the larger type of garden; but if the smaller garden can spare even three yards of room in a corner, yucca will come as a fine surprise on the grand scale in July, and will carry out my contention that you want variety of shape and height to make an aesthetic composition instead of just an amorphous muddle. The yucca, being a child of the desert in Mexico and some of the hotter parts of the United States, such as California, likes the driest possible place and the sunniest, but on the whole accommodates itself very obligingly to our soil and climate.

Ruthless intentions of future discipline

THE FLOWERING SHRUBS and trees are full of especial richness this year, from the common hawthorn in the hedgerows to the treasured beauties in our gardens. They are over all too soon, and it is then, as they begin to fade, that we regret not having kept a record of them in their prime, with a view to possible rearrangements, alterations, eliminations or additions when planting time comes in the autumn. One thinks one will remember, but, in fact, the succession is so rapid and one picture is so quickly replaced by another picture, that our impressions become merged into a blur of colors, shapes, sizes, and seasons. Why, we cry too late, did we not take notes week by week at the time?

It is with a virtuous resolution that I have acquired a large note-book stamped GARDEN RECORDS and four bundles of inch-long labels, with gilt numerals incised on white, from 1 to 100. These, since they are each pierced with a little hole, can be tied to a branch and the corresponding description entered against the number in the notebook. Thus: "No. 10. Shockingly poor washy lilac; destroy; and replace by No. 12." A reference to No. 12 recalls that it is "Fine double-red young lilac; deserves a better place." There comes a moment in the history of every garden when the duds must be scrapped, and the ill-assorted companions separated. My little outfit is by far the most convenient register of such ruthless intentions of future discipline.

A genus of small shrubs which I fancy would never require a removal ticket are the deutzias. Graceful and arching, May-June flowerers, four to six feet, they are ideal for the small garden where space is a consideration. They are easy, do not resent a little lime in the soil; but beware of pruning them if you do not wish to lose the next year's bloom. The most you should do is to cut off the faded sprays and, naturally, take out any dead wood. The only thing to be said against them is that a late frost will damage the flower, and that is a risk which can well be taken.

Summer

The peony is the epitome of June

OFTEN ONE IS ASKED for plants which will flourish
in semi-shade, and in the month of June the noble peony
comes to mind. (I mean the herbaceous sort, not the
species or the tree peony.) It always seems to me that
the herbaceous peony is the very epitome of June. Larger
than any rose, it has something of the cabbage rose's
voluminous quality; and when it finally drops from the
vase, it sheds its vast petticoats with a bump on the table,
all in an intact heap, much as a rose will suddenly fall,
making us look up from our book or conversation, to
notice for one moment the death of what had still appeared to be a living beauty.

To be practical, there is much to recommend the peony.
I will make a list of its virtues. It is a very long-lived plant,
increasing yearly in vigor if you will only leave it un-
disturbed. It likes to stay put. It will, as I said, flourish
in half-shade, and indeed its brag of size and color gains
from the broken light of overhanging branches. It doesn't
object to an alkaline soil, a great advantage to those who
cannot grow lime-hating plants in their garden. Rabbits
do not appear to care for its young shoots. Slugs don't care
for it either; and the only disease it may seriously suffer
from is a fungus, *Botrytis*. If this appears, you must cut
out the diseased bits and burn them; but in the many years
I have grown peonies in my garden I have, touch wood,

never found any trace of disease amongst my gross Edwardian swagger ladies.

The secret of growing the herbaceous peonies is to plant them very shallow and give them a deep, rich run of manure for their roots to find as they go down in search of nourishment. Then they will go ahead, and probably outlive the person who planted them, so that his or her grandchild will be picking finer flowers fifty years hence.

Generous old roses

THESE JUNE EVENINGS, when for once in a way we are allowed a deep warm sloping sunlight, how rare and how precious they are. They ought to be accompanied by fireflies, wild gold flakes in the air, but here we have to make do with tethered flowers instead. Amongst these, the huge lax bushes of the old roses must take an honored place.

The old roses have recently wriggled their way back into favor, and small wonder. They give so little trouble for so great a reward. By the old roses I mean the Cabbage, the Moss, the Centifolias, the Gallicas, the Musks and the Damasks whose very names suggest a honeyed southern dusk.

I know that they have neither the neatness nor the brilliance of the Hybrid Teas, and I know also that most of them suffer from the serious drawback of flowering only once during a season, but what incomparable lavishness they give, while they are about it. There is nothing scrimpy or stingy about them. They have a generosity which is as desirable in plants as in people.

In this revival of the old roses, we surely have rediscovered a form of gardening enjoyed by our Victorian grandparents. I hold in my mind the vision of a rose garden planted in 1870, crammed with old roses that had run about all over the place on their own roots, going into an untidy wilderness, a tangle of roses I could not name. I took a great rosarian with me, and shall never forget her excitement, dashing about, saying that she could not name them either, but must take cuttings in order to preserve these old treasures from loss and destruction.

Fortunately, it is now possible to buy the old roses from some nurserymen who specialize in them. Their catalogs read like one long poem of names: Reine des Violettes, Cardinal Richelieu, Nuits de Young, Tuscany, *Rosa mundi,* the striped pink-and-white rose, which many people confuse with the York and Lancaster. There are so many of them that it is not possible for me to give more than a brief suggestion about what to plant if you have the space to afford in your garden.

The provenance of delphiniums

IF WE WERE LEFT with only one kind of herbaceous perennial the delphinium would have to rank very high in the list of choices, especially today when the variety of color and the magnificence of the spikes far excel the somewhat monotonous and spindly specimens that satisfied us in the old herbaceous border. Not that I aspire to grow such monsters as were intended for the flower show and had to be left behind because they would not fit into the horse-box provided for their transport. It is the color rather than the size which attracts me, the astonishing range of blues now available, and also those "shot" mixtures of blue with lavender and almost pink, like watered silk, and also the lovely whites of the Giant Pacific strain with their black eyes looking at you, seriously as it were, from the center of the huge, pure florets.

I have now received some literature on the subject of the delphinium, containing information some of which was new to me in my ignorance. In the hope that others may be equally ignorant, and equally interested, I pass some of it on. It concerns the origins of this splendid plant, the mystery of the garden hybrids, the methods of propagation, and advice as to cultivation. When I add that this pamphlet is written by Mr. Allan Langdon, its authority will scarcely be called into question.

I am always fascinated by the provenance of our garden plants. It is surely romantic to think that our cherished and coddled treasures are the wildings of some remote valley or mountainside in Asia, Africa, or America. Not only wildings but weeds. . . .

I did know that the distribution of the delphinium was world wide, but until I read Mr. Langdon's pamphlet I did not realize how truly world wide it was. It ranges from California to Tibet and China, crossing the Alps and moving eastwards into Russia, Persia, Kashmir, Sikkim, wandering up into the foothills of Himalaya and wandering down into Abyssinia and Kenya. What a geographical journey: you have to cover half the globe to follow it, picking up wild delphiniums all along the way.

These wild delphiniums, these natives, bear little resemblance to the delphinium as we know it. The evolution of our garden hybrid is unknown and unexplained. Mr. Langdon states his opinion that a chancy fertilization gave rise to the beginnings of the superb towering spires of blue, proportionately tall as the spire of Salisbury Cathedral rising into the English summer air. He thinks that the species known as *Delphinium elatum* was probably a parent, and another source of information apprises me that this species extends from the Pyrenees to Mongolia. As Mr. Langdon rightly remarks—and who should know better—this absence of genealogical ancestry has not lightened the task of modern hybridists, and surely he justifies his claim that they have nevertheless produced "the most beautiful of all herbaceous plants," indeed, "very considerably enhanced, for none of the species has anything approaching the stature of our modern hybrid." They are, he says, of little value, being inconspicuous and unattractive. In plain English, they are dull, meager things, whereas no one could accuse the modern development of the delphinium of being inconspicuous. It is eminently conspicuous.

Meanwhile, put a handful of very coarse ashes over every crown as a protection against slugs and thin out all weak shoots. The fewer shoots you have to each root, the finer spike you will get.

A man who collects baths

I KNOW A MAN who collects baths. He buys broken-down baths at almost no cost at local auction sales and buries them in his garden, with the wastehole open and a thick layer of coke-clinker or some similar rough stuff underneath to ensure drainage. He then fills the bath up to the rim with whatever kind of soil he requires; covers the rim over to hide it; and there he is, with a securely insulated patch in which to grow his choosy plants.

I am not suggesting that our gardens should all become a submerged cemetery for obsolete baths, but it does seem to me a helpful idea for people who have a difficult soil to cope with—people who want to grow things that will not consent to flourish in the soil with which they have been blessed or cursed. The dwellers on chalk, for example, who wish to grow the lime-hating gentians, could overcome their difficulty. The dwellers on clay would find that the indestructible, uncontrollable clay could be eliminated in favor of a soft bed suitable to peat-loving subjects. Again, if you want a swampy bit of ground for moisture-loving primulas, you can create it, very suitably, in the buried bath. Again, if you have a flinty soil, which throws up flints over and over again from the bottom, however often you may think you have cleared them out, you can replace that spiteful bit of ground with a richer loam, controlled and contained within the rectangular shape of the sunken bath.

It is an idea lending itself to much expansion.

Peruvian lilies are oddly named

THE PERUVIAN LILIES, or *Alstroemerias*, are rather oddly named since they all come from Chile or Brazil. Now in mid-June they are just coming into flower, and should be at their best during the next two or three weeks, so this is the time to see them and judge for yourself. The common old rather dingy form, *A. aurantiaca*, is no longer worth growing, when you can have such superb varieties as the Ligtu hybrids, which burst into every shade of color from a strawy buff to a coral rose, and apart from their garden value are among the loveliest of flowers for picking, since they not only arrange themselves in graceful curves in water but last for an unusually long time. A bed of *Alstroemeria* Ligtu hybrids in full sun is a glowing sight.

May I insist on two or three points for growing them, dictated to me by practical experience? First, grow them from seed, sown on the spot where you wish them to continue their existence. This is because the roots are extremely brittle, and they loathe being transplanted. So suspicious are they of transplantation that even seedlings carefully tipped out of pots seem to sense that something precarious and unsettling is happening to them, and resent it in the unanswerable way of plants by the simple protest of death. Second, sow them either when the seed is freshly harvested, or, better still, in early spring. Third, sow them in a sunny, well-drained place. Fourth, cover them over with some protective litter for the first winter. After observing all these instructions you will not have to worry about them any more, beyond staking them with twiggy sticks as soon as they reappear every year six inches above the ground, for the stems are fragile and easily broken down by wind or heavy rain. You will find that the clumps increase in size and beauty, with self-sown seedlings coming up all over the near neighborhood.

An obliging iris

IT SUDDENLY STRUCK ME that an odd omission had occurred during the years I have been writing on gardening: I seem never to have done sufficient justice to *Iris sibirica*. This forgetfulness must have been a form of ingratitude. There is a nasty element in human nature which takes for granted the obliging, accommodating, serviceable character of some people and forgets to render thanks.

I would like to repair the omission and render thanks now to this graceful iris which arises from reedy stems in delicate flower-heads of dark purple, lavender, and white. It varies in its color, and that is one of its most attractive characteristics. If you hold it up against the light, you will perceive its delicate veining.

It is the easiest of things to grow, for it will do well by the waterside in a fairly damp bed, although it does not like being drowned under water all the year round. It will

do equally well in an ordinary bed or border; in fact, it
will do its best for us anywhere, even to the extent of
seeding itself and appearing in unexpected places, as I
have recently noticed in my own garden.

I say "recently," because I was astonished to find *Iris
sibirica* flowering in corners where I knew I had never
deliberately planted it, and could not imagine how it had
come there, until I discovered that the seedlings of this
iris take no longer than two years to reach their flowering
stage. The seedlings would not necessarily come true to
the color of their parents, but one might always have the
luck to raise a particularly good form. From this reason it
would be worth while growing a drill of home-saved seed
in an unwanted strip of ground and seeing what would
result after two years' waiting.

The same may be said of that exquisite relation of *Iris
sibirica*, the almost black little *Iris chrysographes*. It also
will flower from seed within two years. It comes from
China and is perhaps a plant for the connoisseur rather
than for the amateur gardener who just wants the mass
effect he will gain more readily from the tall and slender
sibirica. Iris chrysographes grows only a foot high and
needs looking close into for a full perception of its beauty.
Yet it is quite easy to grow, given a place that never dries
out and is rich in humus.

Still, *Iris sibirica* is for everyone, forming large clumps
of perhaps rather untidy leaves, whose untidiness is re-
deemed by the wealth of tall flowers rising in June and
persisting for several weeks as the buds succeed one
another in their opening.

A vertical garden

NEW YORK, so we are told, could not spread sideways beyond a certain area owing to the geological formations on which that astonishing city has arisen. It had to go vertically towards the sky because it could not spread horizontally across the land. This curious and interesting fact accounts for that most original form of architecture, the skyscraper. No one had even thought of building skyscrapers before, because there was no need to. There had always been plenty of ground room.

Now in small gardens there is not always as much ground room as the gardener greedily wants, and I saw recently in the relatively small garden of a friend a most ingenious idea for getting herself out of the cramped difficulty. She had been given a flat flower bed to deal with, but instead of leaving it just flat and restricted in space, she had built it up into little terraces with rough stones; three stories high, and into these little stone-walled terraces she had packed and crammed every kind of plant that enjoys good drainage conditions: pinks, thrift, campanulas, lewisias, violas, all ordinary things, but so effective grown in tiers as she was growing them, in a foaming mass and fall of flower and color. You see the idea? You get the benefit three ways. You get the stone-walling, you get the flat bits under the stone-walling, and then on the top you get a wide expanse of bed in which you can plant anything you like. You will, by this means, have increased your garden space threefold.

Apart from the gain in space, it is always amusing to try experiments with plants in a dry wall, even though that wall may not be more than two stones high. Many plants will flourish which otherwise would perish from

the damp of our climate. When they can get their roots back between stones they seem to tuck themselves in and preserve themselves from rot. We do not need to build a skyscraper: we need only two rows of stone to pack our Cheddar pink into, let us say, or some of the Allwood pinks which sometimes prove disappointing grown in an ordinary border.

Ixias are a God-given present in June

BRAVE GARDENERS who have a sunny corner to spare, at the foot of a south wall for choice, and a poor sandy soil, should plant some bulbs of Ixia, the South African corn-lily. It is a graceful thing, about eighteen inches high, with rush-like leaves and a flower spike in various colors: white, yellow, coral pink, and sometimes striped like the boiled sweets of our childhood. There is also a particularly lovely and rather strange variety, green with a black center, *Ixia viridiflora*.

Ixias are not entirely hardy, though hardier than the freesias which they somewhat resemble. Very sharp drainage, deep planting of about six inches, and a cover throughout winter should, however, ensure their survival, and those which fail to reappear can be replaced annually. Of course, the more you can plant, the better. They flower in June and take up very little room. They are ideal for picking, as they last a long time in water and arrange themselves with thin and slender elegance in a tall glass.

They do also very well as pot plants in a cold greenhouse or a conservatory, not requiring any heat but only protection from frost. If you grow them this way, you must disregard the advice to plant them six inches deep, and cover them with only an inch or so of soil—sandy loam and a handful of leaf mold mixed to each pot, and crocks for drainage at the bottom.

I do hope you will order some Ixias. I admit that they

are apt to die out after a year or so; but to those gardeners who have a poor, starved soil and a warm corner they are a God-given present in June.

The astonishing growth of certain roses

I AM ASTONISHED, and even alarmed, by the growth which certain roses will make in the course of a few years. There is one called Madame Plantier, which we planted at the foot of a worthless old apple tree, vaguely hoping that it might cover a few feet of the trunk. Now it is fifteen feet high with a girth of fifteen yards, tapering towards the top like the waist of a Victorian beauty and pouring down in a vast crinoline stitched all over with its white sweet-scented clusters of flower.

Madame Plantier dates back, in fact, to 1835, just two years before Queen Victoria came to the throne, so she and the Queen may be said to have grown up together towards the crinolines of their maturity. Queen Victoria is dead, but Madame Plantier is still very much alive. I go out to look at her in the moonlight: she gleams, a pear-shaped ghost, contriving to look both matronly and virginal. She has to be tied up round her tree, in long strands, otherwise she would make only a big straggly bush; we have found that the best method is to fix a sort of tripod of bean-poles against the tree and tie the strands to that.

Another favorite white rose of mine is Paul's Lemon Pillar. It should not be called white. A painter might see it as greenish, suffused with sulphur yellow, and its great merit lies not only in the vigor of its growth and wealth of flowering, but also in the perfection of its form. The shapeliness of each bud has a sculptural quality which suggests curled shavings of marble, if one may imagine marble made of the softest ivory suede. The full-grown flower is scarcely less beautiful; and when the first explosion of bloom is over, a carpet of thick white petals covers the ground, so dense as to look as though it had been deliberately laid.

The old Madame Alfred Carrière is likewise in full flower. Smaller than Paul's rose, and with no pretensions to a marmoreal shape, Madame Alfred, white, flushed with shell pink, has the advantage of a sweet, true-rose scent, and will grow to the eaves of any reasonably proportioned house, even on a west or north wall.

Remembered delight of mertensia

MENTALLY SURVEYING some of the delights of spring, which are already over, I recalled with gratitude the Virginian cowslip, *Mertensia virginica*. Some American visitors strolling round my garden stopped to gaze at it in distrustful surprise. To them it was a weed, and for a moment I thought they were going to show their helpfulness by pulling it up. Thus do we often fail to remember that the treasures of our own gardens are the weeds of other lands. The Japanese, after all, always ate the bulbs of *Lilium auratum,* scale by scale, after the manner of a globe artichoke, until they discovered that the European market esteemed the wild bulb of Mount Fujiyama for its flower.

My Americans had just been enraptured by their first sight of an English bluebell wood; and when I remarked that the *Mertensia* smothering its native woodland must be every bit as beautiful, they gaped at me as though I had said something paradoxical. They evidently thought me daft for cherishing six poor plants of a thing they were accustomed to see growing by the acre. My pleasure in my *Mertensia* was not thereby diminished. A lovely sky blue, with gray-green leaves, it had been flowering for weeks, from the middle of April right up to the end of May, in the broken light of a corner under some cobnuts, for although it will thrive equally well in sun it is one of those useful things which really prefer the shade. What it does insist on is a loose, leafy soil with some sand, or a peaty soil; and since the two- to three-foot stems are rather brittle, it is advisable to support them with a few twiggy sticks, otherwise they flop and sometimes snap. Do not be alarmed if it starts to look very miserable in June. It is not dead, but merely dying down according to its nature. It will reappear next year.

I cannot imagine why the Americans should call it a cowslip. Cowslips, as we all know, are yellow, and belong to the great family of primulas, whereas the *Mertensia* of Virginia is as blue as our own naturalized comfrey, and indeed belongs to the same botanical family as the comfrey, the *Boraginaceae.*

Familiar prettiness

THE MORE ONE GARDENS, the more one learns; and the more one learns, the more one realizes how little one knows. I suppose the whole of life is like that: the endless complications, the endless difficulties, the endless fight against one thing or another, whether it be green-fly on the roses or the complexity of personal relationships.

I was thinking about wistaria, the old mauve kind, because its obvious prettiness reminded me of picture postcards and riverside tea gardens. One should perhaps not allow oneself to be susceptible to cheap associations, and should consider any plant in relation only to its own beauty, regardless of botanical snobbery, but however conscientiously one may endeavor to preserve an objective attitude, it is sometimes difficult not to be influenced. I do, for instance, try very hard to look at aubretia as though I were seeing it for the first and not the millionth time. Also at laburnum, surely the most fairy-tale tree, with its golden rain, dripping in becalmed fireworks which never drift in blackened cinders to the ground.

These things, the aubretia and the laburnum and the wistaria, all came into the same category in my mind, making me wonder what one could do about them to redeem them from their common use. And then I suddenly saw a wistaria that I must have planted years ago, and had forgotten. It had grown right up to a fig tree and had struggled its way upwards towards the light, and was suddenly pouring itself downwards to meet a clematis called The President, with large mauve flowers exactly matching.

One gets surprises of that sort, compensating the disappointments.

All the same, to conclude this discussion, may I suggest that you should plant the *white* wistaria? It is not often seen, but can be obtained from most good nurseries. A truly lovely thing, so purely white, like a waterfall or sea-spray foaming.

The temperamental gentian

VISITORS TO THE CHELSEA flower show may have noticed a large platform or billiard table entirely planted with *Gentiana acaulis*. Billiard tables are usually green, but this one was blue. The deep yet brilliant color of those trumpets, raised motionless in a fanfare of blue music, must have aroused envy in many hearts.

Perhaps one should hesitate to recommend so temperamental a plant. It is said, for instance, that *G. acaulis* will flower freely on one side of a path but not on the other, for no apparent reason; and certainly the advice given by successful growers is bewildering in its variety. Reginald Farrer believed in a rich diet; feed it, he said, on old boots, pig-trough garbage, and the blood of kings. Other people will tell you to stamp on it; others, again, that where a particular little cress-like weed flourishes, there also will the gentian thrive. Two things seem certain: that it dislikes drought at the roots, taking the usual revenge if you allow it to get parched; and that you must try it in different places until you find the right place. I have had three shots at it myself, and at last it seems pleased, though I cannot yet rival the gentleman who replied modestly to Farrer's inquiry by saying that he "did not think he had much more than five miles of it." A statement which, upon investigation, turned out to be true.

For the comfort of gardeners on an alkaline soil, it may be added that *G. acaulis* is a lime-lover, unlike the September-flowering gentian *sino-ornata*, which dies instantly at one distant sniff of lime. Mortar-rubble, with its natural content of a lot of lime, and a top-dressing of bonemeal are both gratefully received by *G. acaulis*. And for the further comfort of gardeners who want a patch of gentians, not necessarily five miles long, in their garden, and who want to depend on an August display, *Gentiana septemfida* is probably the best and easiest to grow. *Septemfida*, by the way, has nothing to do with September, although it sounds like it; "*septemfida*" merely means "cleaved into seven divisions." This gentian wants a peaty, loamy, leaf-moldy bed; and hates getting parched.

Garden ornaments

A CORRESPONDENT SUGGESTS that I might write about garden ornaments. I am grateful for this idea, which indeed had occurred to me before now, but which I shrank from in the fear of offending some readers' susceptibilities. There must be many people who cherish a deep affection for their synthetic stone gnomes, toadstools, rabbits, elves, cherubs, and bird baths ornamented with sipping doves. Far be it from me to subvert their innocent pleasure. It is all a matter of taste, and we cannot all be expected to share the same tastes.

Nevertheless, I feel that my correspondent is on the right lines. She wants to know what I would suggest as some piece of focal ornament in the average small garden. Her own choice would be for "something classical or antique," but she wonders if this would not look somewhat pretentious, apart from any question of cost. I do not think it would. I feel quite sure that it is better to invest in something of good design, say a little statue or a fluted column often to be picked up for a small price in a stonemason's yard, than to spend money on the synthetic stone or concrete of the manufacturer's catalog. For instance, I once bought two charming life-size eighteenth-century statues of a boy and a girl for almost nothing, in a junk shop. Then again, I rescued an old laundry copper, lying discarded in a patch of nettles. A vast thing, of the most beautiful green color, it might well be mistaken for some Egyptian bronze of inestimable age and value. I got it for nothing, "if you like to take the trouble of carrying it away."

Then there are sundials. I rather like sundials, in spite of what Hilaire Belloc wrote on one of them:

I am a sundial, and I make a botch
Of what is done far better by a watch.

They must be plain and straightforward, not arty-crafty; be functional; be placed not as a mere adornment, but where they will fulfil their duty, however puzzled the poor things may get by summertime.

Herbaceous borders have had their day

ONE OF THESE DAYS I must cope with what once tried to be an herbaceous border, but which is now a mess and a compromise. Herbaceous borders, perhaps, have had their day. They require to be immaculately kept and elaborately planned if they are to give their best; no pleasure can be derived from a jumble of plants, stuck in irrespective of color or character, flopping after rain, prostrate after a sudden gale, tousled, sodden, leaning sideways at all angles, delphiniums in the back row, lupine and phlox in the middle, catmint and pinks along the front . . . one is only too familiar with these survivals of Edwardian times.

The question of staking is always a difficult one. Twiggy peasticks, pushed in at an early stage of the growth, are preferable to a stockade of bamboos hastily added as an afterthought when heads become top-heavy: peasticks will be hidden and covered over, as bamboos never will. I was told recently of an ingenious method for supporting perennial subjects in the border. In the idle, indoor days of winter you employ your leisure making large circles of stout wire, crisscrossing them with thinner wire into, say, four sections, meeting in a sort of hub at the middle;

you then supply a central pole, of metal if you can get it, say bits of an old railing, more durable than wood. In the spring you start your wire circle a few inches from the ground, raising it gradually up the central pole as the height of the plant increases, and as the plant grows up through the sections. I thought to myself that one might improve on the idea by placing two or more of the wire circles round the pole, according to the eventual height expected of the plant; this would save keeping a constant watch to see if the circle needed raising, and would also afford a double support to brittle stems.

It would entail a good deal of winter work, neat fingers, a pair of wire-cutters, a pair of pincers, and a couple of rolls of wire, thick and thin; but you would then have a fixture to last without renewal for many years. Even if you have not got an herbaceous border properly speaking, it should be a useful hint applied to any special treasure of a plant, too snappy and too tall to carry its own weight in high summer. All the same, I foresee that my border will soon become a border of flowering shrubs and the shrubby types of rose, with a solitary delphinium, over-looked in the background, to remind me of what the unlamented herbaceous border once was.

A true myrtle

I HAVE A MYRTLE growing on a wall. It is only the common myrtle, *Myrtus communis*, but I think you would have to travel far afield to find a lovelier shrub for July and August flowering. The small, pointed, dark-green leaves are smothered at this time of year by a mass of white flowers with quivering centers of the palest green yellow, so delicate in their white and gold that it appears as though a cloud of butterflies had alighted on the dark shrub.

The myrtle is a plant full of romantic associations in mythology and poetry, the sacred emblem of Venus and of love, though why Milton called it brown I never could understand, unless he was referring to the fact that the leaves, which are by way of being evergreen, do turn brown in frosty weather or under a cold wind. Even if it gets cut down in winter there is nothing to worry about, for it springs up again, at any rate in the south. In the north it might be grateful for a covering of ashes or fir branches over the roots. It strikes very easily from cuttings, and a plant in a pot is a pretty thing to possess, especially if it can be stood near the housedoor, where the aromatic leaves may be pinched as you go in and out. In very mild sections it should not require the protection of a wall, but may be grown as a bush or small tree in the open, or even, which I think should be most charming of all, into a small grove suggestive of Greece and her nymphs.

The flowers are followed by little inky berries, which in their turn are quite decorative, and would probably grow if you sowed a handful of them.

In this connection, I might mention the bog myrtle, though it is not really a myrtle except in common parlance. By some people it might be regarded as a weed, but for its strong, resinous scent, which gives it its second lovely name, sweet gale; it is well worth bringing in, if you come across it, and giving a place in a rough corner, where it will catch the prevailing wind. It does, however, exact a purely acid soil, as peaty as possible, so is of no use to the dwellers on chalk or lime. The more moisture it gets the better, when it will spread by means of its underground roots. Travelers across Dartmoor may remember getting unexpected whiffs, like passing through a pine forest on a warm day.

Full-bosomed trollop of a rose

THE OTHER DAY I encountered a gentleman wearing amber-colored spectacles. He was kind enough to say that I had a well-chosen range of color in my garden. I expressed some surprise at this, since it was obvious that he could not be seeing any colors in their true color, but must be seeing them in some fantastic alteration of tincture. Yes, he said, of course I do; it amuses me; try my glasses on, he said; look at your roses; look also at your brown-tiled roofs; look at the clouds in the sky. Look, he said, handing them to me. I looked, and was instantly transferred into a different world. A volcanic eruption, or possibly an earthquake, seemed imminent. Alarming, perhaps, but how strange, how magical.

Everything had become intensified. All the greens of turf or trees had deepened. All the blues were cut out, or turned to a blackish brown. The whites turned to a rich buttercup yellow. The most extraordinary effect of all was when you switched over to the pink variations of color. There has been some correspondence in the press recently about that old favorite rose, Zéphyrine Drouhin. Dear though she was to me, perfect in scent, vigorous in growth, magnificent in *floraison* (a lovely and expressive word we might well import from French into English, since we seem to have no equivalent in our language), and so kindly and obliging in having no thorns, never a cross word or a scratch as one picked her—dear though she was, I say, I had always deplored the crude pink of her complexion. It was her only fault. Seen through the magic glasses, she turned into a copper orange; burnished; incredible.

Zéphyrine Drouhin has a romantic history, worthy of her breeze-like name. She derives from a hybrid found growing in 1817 in a hedge of roses in the Ile de Bourbon, now called Réunion, off the east coast of Africa. This hybrid became the parent of the whole race of Bourbon roses, which in their turn have given rise to the modern roses we call Hybrid Perpetuals and Hybrid Teas. This is putting it very briefly, and seems to bear no relation to the great pink bush flowering in the summer garden under the name Zéphyrine Drouhin. Who was Zéphyrine? Who was Monsieur Drouhin? These are questions I cannot answer. They sound like characters in a novel by Flaubert. I know only that this gentle, thornless, full-bosomed, generous trollop of a rose turned into a fabulous flaming bush under the sorcery of the tinted glasses.

In place of herbaceous borders

PLAINTIVE LETTERS reach me saying that if I do not like herbaceous borders what would I put in their place? It is quite true that I have no great love for herbaceous borders or for the plants that usually fill them—coarse things with no delicacy or quality about them. I think the only justification for such borders is that they shall be perfectly planned, both in regard to color and to grouping; perfectly staked; and perfectly weeded. How many people have the time or the labor? The alternative is a border largely composed of flowering shrubs, including the big bush roses; but for those who still desire a mixed border it is possible to design one which will (more or less) look after itself once it has become established.

It could be carried out in various color schemes. Here is an idea for one in red and purple and pink: Polyantha roses Dusky Maiden, Frensham, Donald Prior; Musk roses Pink Prosperity, Cornelia, Felicia, Vanity; the common old red herbaceous peonies, with Darwin tulips planted amongst them if you like; and a front edging of the dwarf asters and daisies such as Dresden China which make big mats and go on for ever, and even violets for early flowering, and some patches of the ornamental strawberry with bright red fruits all through the summer. Nor would I despise a counterpane, at intervals, of *Cotoneaster horizontalis*, crawling over the ground with its herringbone spine, its small box-like leaves of darkest green and its brilliantly red berries in autumn.

Another idea, pale and rather ghostly, a twilight-moonlight border. Forsythia along the back; Musk roses Danae, Moonlight, and Thisbe in the middle; evening primroses, *Oenothera biennis*, self-sowing; *Iris ochroleuca*, tall and white and yellow; creamy peonies; and a front carpet of silver-foliaged artemisias and stachys.

Of course, these are only the roughest indications, outlines to be filled in. The main thing, it seems to me, is to have a foundation of large, tough, untroublesome plants with intervening spaces for the occupation of annuals, bulbs, or anything that takes your fancy. The initial outlay would seem extravagant, but at least it would not have to be repeated, and the effect would improve with every year.

Foxtail lilies, aristocrats of the garden

VISITORS TO JUNE and July flower shows may have been surprised, pleased, and puzzled by enormous spikes, six to eight feet in height, which looked something like a giant lupine, but which, on closer inspection, proved to be very different. They were to be seen in various colors: pale yellow, buttercup yellow, greenish yellow, white and greenish white, pink, and a curious fawn pink which is as hard to describe, because as subtle, as the color of a chaffinch's breast.

These were *Eremuri*, sometimes called the foxtail lily

and sometimes the giant asphodel. They belong, in fact, to the botanical family of the lilies, but, unlike most lilies, they do not grow from a bulb. They grow from a star-fish-like root, which is brittle and needs very careful handling when you transplant it. I think this is probably the reason why some people fail to establish the foxtail lily satisfactorily. It should be moved in the last weeks of September or the first weeks of October, and it should be moved with the least possible delay. The roots should never be allowed to wait, shriveling, out of the ground. Plant them instantly, as soon as they arrive from the nursery. Spread out the roots, flat, in a rather rich loamy soil, and cover them over to protect them from frost during their first winter. Plant them under the shelter of a hedge, if you can; they dislike a strong wind, and the magnificence of their spires will show up better for the backing of a dark hedge. They like lime and sunshine.

Thus established, the foxtail lily should give increasing delight as the years go by. They get better and better as they grow older, throwing up more and more spires of flower from each crown of their starfish root. There are several sorts obtainable: the giant *Eremurus robustus*, which flowers in June, and then the smaller ones, the Shelford hybrids and the Warei hybrids in their strange colors. Splendid things; torches of pale color, towering, dwarfing the ordinary little annuals. Aristocrats of the garden, they are well worth their cost.

It sometimes pays to treat plants rough

AFTER MANY LONG docile years of following all the advice given me by professional gardeners and by the authoritative authors of gardening books, I have turned insubordinate. I have discovered for myself that it some-

times pays to treat plants rough; to go against the rules and get a surprising reward. The odd thing is—and everything is odd in gardening, unless, I suppose, you do it with all the resources of horticultural science, and know all about chromosomes and hormones—the odd thing is that often sheer necessity teaches us the lesson.

Thus, a self-sown broom came up in my garden.

It grew vigorously, as self-sown seedlings will, but it had not put itself where I wanted it. It was smothering a peony which I particularly esteemed. Reluctant to uproot it altogether, as it had been giving a fine display in its wrong place, I took the shears to it and chopped recklessly, with the remark that if it survived so much the better for it, and if it died so much the worse. Far from dying it grows more vigorously than ever. I now have recourse to the pruning shears about once a fortnight. Had it been a precious thing, cosseted and cherished, I should never have dared to mishandle it so unkindly. Only indifference to its fate lets me so wildly loose upon it.

Do not imagine that I am advocating an experimental treatment for precious shrubs. One must try one's experiments on the things one doesn't much mind about, and ill-treat them as I am now ill-treating our English grammar. Chop the things you don't want and you will find that they respond, even as my self-sown broom responded.

Experiments sometimes pay high dividends. There was a revolutionary idea put forward in recent years that roses should be pruned during the dormant months of winter, instead of at the orthodox time in late March when the sap must be rising. This seemed a common-sensible contention; and so it seems to have been proved.

I shall go on going against the rules. That is the only way one can learn.

The peculiar psychology of daphne

NOW IN JULY the bushes of mezereon, or *Daphne mezereum*, should be hung with their fruits, if the birds have not already pecked them off. It is well worth while to save and sow some of them, for they germinate very freely and a crop of young plants is the result. I am told on good authority that the daphne is not very long-lived but has a better expectation of life when it is growing on its own roots, i.e. has not been grafted, so the moral of growing it from seed (or cuttings) is obvious.

The mezereon seems to share with the Madonna lily a predilection for cottage gardens. Bushes five feet high and four feet wide carry their wine-colored bloom on the naked stems year after year in early spring in a luxuriance unknown to grander gardens where far more trouble is taken about them. Cottagers apparently just stick it in everywhere, when, with the perversity of an inverted snobbishness, it grows. It is useless to try to explain this peculiar psychology of certain plants. One must accept it and do the best one can to reproduce the conditions they appear to enjoy.

After struggling for years to induce *Daphne mezereum* to thrive in my garden, I have at last achieved a miserable degree of success by planting it in a mixture of leaf mold and sand, in the broken shade of some trees of Kentish cobnuts. This is the treatment I would recommend: a spongy soil with overhead shade in summer. After all, the mezereon is sometimes claimed as a native of Britain, growing in woods, so it seems reasonable to plant it in the sort of soil it would be likely to encounter in its natural habitat, full of decayed leaves and humus, rich with the fallen wealth of centuries.

On the other hand, some people will tell you that it never thrives better than in a hot, dry place, such as a gravelly path right up against the house. So what is one to believe?

There are two kinds of *Daphne mezereum*. One is the familiar claret-colored one, pink as a *Vin Rosé* held up to the light in a *carafe*. The other is white, *Daphne mezereum alba*. They have different-colored berries. The familiar one has bright red berries. The white form has bright yellow berries. I would strongly advise you to poke some seeds of both into small pots, instead of letting the birds have them. Daphnes do not transplant well, and should always be tipped straight out of a pot, like a clematis.

I have not observed seed on any of the other daphnes, but there is a prostrate one called *D. blagayana*, ivory in color and intensely sweet-scented in the early spring. This likes to be layered and weighted down with stones at every point where the layer has been inserted. It will then spread outwards into a mat of fresh growth, which may eventually attain a width of six feet or more. It is a delight to pick on cold days, to bring into the warmth of a room when the honeyed smell floats round into stray corners with a suggestion of bees and summer airs. The same is true of *Daphne odora*, but that unfortunately is not quite hardy and needs the protection of glass throughout the frosty months, either in a greenhouse or under a cloche.

The village flower show

IN THE SUMMER DAYS before the war, the village flower show, which would be better called a produce show, was quite a grand affair. There were two marquees, large enough to dwarf the Miniature-Gardens-on-Plates and the Victorian-Posy-in-an-Egg-Cup into looking even tinier. The local nurserymen staged handsome exhibits *Not for competition,* raising the standard and causing the Amateurs-without-help (Class A), the Amateurs-with-help (Class B), and the Cottagers (Class C) to exclaim "Coo, look at that!" determined that next year at the show they would try to emulate their professional neighbors.

Those good days disappeared for a time; the village could no longer afford marquees, and had to arrange its show, more modestly, in any shelter it could get: the women's club, the parish room of the church, or a barn borrowed from a farmer. It had to be staged somehow or somewhere, to keep the show going and to prevent interest from dying out.

Now, better days are returning. Marquees have reappeared, and the big nurserymen are again willing to show their wares. The sumptuous effect of the Best Box of Vegetables again graces the trestle tables and how magnificent they are in shape and color, those mixed collections of red tomatoes, orange carrots, ivory parsnips, pale potatoes freshly washed in milk, jade-green lettuce, blood-red beetroot, and emerald peas, with one pod split open.

How fine, indeed, in their assembly are the fruits of the earth, simply, and by cottagers, displayed. Great hairy gooseberries set out on kitchen plates; black currants the size of marbles; raspberries like pink thimbles made for a giantess; and some soft peaches and brown figs from the greenhouse of an Amateur-with-help. How rural are the eggs, the bunches of herbs, the home-made cakes, the colored jars of jam, the golden honey. How pretty the baskets of mixed flowers, and how touching the jam-pots of wild flowers and grasses collected by the children.

Everyone comes in clothes that seem to match the exhibits: flowered frocks, bright scarves, and here and there a sunbonnet. The children have been scrubbed until their cheeks shine. One knows that they are little scamps really, but today you could not convince even a police-man that they had ever climbed the gate into an orchard. There are some speeches, and everybody says something amiable about everybody else; local feuds are forgotten for the day. There is no ill feeling when the red, blue, and green tickets meaning first, second, and third prizes have been hopefully inspected on the cards, nor any grievance against the glum silence of no ticket at all, for it is recognized that the judges have been fair and im-partial. Someone is in charge of a phonograph, and in the evening after the prizes have been distributed there may be some dancing in the field outside. The corn is ripening down in the valley; the young moon hangs over the church tower, and a little breeze springs up to ruffle the leaves of the poplars.

I love the village flower show; I prefer it even to the

village fête, or *feet* as they usually pronounce it. This has a holiday tang about it, with a loudspeaker van blaring away, and squalid litter left blowing about somebody's garden. What I like about the show is its complete lack of self-consciousness. Here is no organized entertainment: no folk-dancing at 5 P.M. which might once have been spontaneous but now certainly isn't, except in a few remote villages; no one selling raffle tickets for a bottle of whisky; no pot-shots taken with darts at the effigy of some unpopular foreign dictator. The village show is honest-to-God, whatever that may mean, and I think it does mean something. It means honest work and long experience, no nonsense about green fingers, which is one of the most slipshod, easygoing, indulgent expressions ever invented. Ask any gardener or farmer what he thinks of it, and you will be rewarded as you deserve by a slow cynical grin and no verbal answer at all, except possibly "Green fingers, my foot!"

He knows better. He knows that hard digging, rich feeding, deep knowledge, and constant care are the only way to produce the prize-winning exhibits he puts on to the trestle tables at his annual local show, for the admiration and esteem of his neighbors in competition.

There is no short cut to success in prize-taking, or to the silver trophy which has to be won three years running for the best exhibit on points and which will eventually stand between the pair of Staffordshire china dogs on the mantelpiece in the front parlor, suitably inscribed with the name of the winner, a record of triumph, and (one hopes) an incentive to his children and grandchildren for many years to come.

Plants that take happily to shade

PEOPLE OFTEN ASK what plants are suitable for a shady situation, by which they mean either the north side of a wall or house, or in the shadow cast by trees. There are so many such plants that no one need despair. A number of shrubby things will do well, such as the azaleas, the laurels, the rhododendrons, and a pretty, seldom seen, low-growing shrub with waxy white pendent flowers called *Zenobia pulverulenta*, always provided that the soil is lime-free for all these subjects. The many cotoneasters and barberries have no objection to shade, and are less pernickety as to soil. *Viburnum burkwoodii* will thrive, very easy and sweet-scented, making a big bush. The well-known snowberry will grow anywhere and is attractive in autumn with its ivory berries and tangle of black twigs. And if you want something more choice than the snowberry, there are many magnolias which enjoy the protection of a north wall: *M. lennei*, wine-pink; *M. soulangeana*, white; and *M. liliflora nigra*, a deep claret color, which has the advantage of a very long flowering season, all through May and June, with a few odd flowers appearing even in July and August. The magnolias all appreciate peat moss or leaf mold to fill in the hole you dig out when you plant them, and it is important not to let them suffer from drought before they have had time to become established.

If, however, you have no space for these rather large shrubs, there are plenty of things other than shrubs to fill up an un-sunny border. There are the foxgloves, which can now be obtained in varieties far superior to the woodland foxglove, flowering all round the stem, and in colors preferable to the old magenta, lovely though that may look in the woods. The Excelsior strain flowers all round. The columbines will also tolerate shade, and there is a charming old plant called *Astrantia*, the masterwort, seldom seen now except in cottage gardens, which will ramp away in an unpromising shady place and increase itself by seed. The *Epimediums* should not be overlooked; they make clumps of pretty foliage and throw up delicate sprays of flower like tiny orchids in May. The hellebores and the lily of the valley, the primroses and the polyanthus, the candelabra primulas, and, as you grow more ambitious, the blue poppy *Meconopsis baileyi*, which is the dream of every gardener, will all take happily to a shaded home, especially if some moisture keeps them fresh.

Where did Gabriel get a lily?

A LOT OF PEOPLE have a lot of trouble with lilies. I have myself. I try. I fail. I despair. Then I try again. Only last week did it occur to me to go and ask for advice from a famous grower of lilies in my neighborhood, which was the obvious and sensible thing to do. I might have thought of it before. Surely he will not mind my passing on the hints he gave me, especially if it leads to an encouragement to grow some varieties of this supremely beautiful family.

There are four cardinal points, he said, like the compass. Point 1: good drainage is essential; no stagnant moisture, even if it means digging out a hole and putting a layer of crocks or coarse clinker at the bottom. Point 2: make up a suitable bed to receive your bulbs, a bed rich in humus, which means leaf mold, peat moss, compost, or whatever form you can command. Point 3: never plant lily bulbs which have been out of the ground too long or have had their basal roots cut off. Reject these, even if you find them offered at cheap rates in the horticultural department of some chain stores. Lily bulbs should be lifted fresh and replanted quickly, with their basal roots intact; therefore it is advisable to obtain them from any reputable nurseryman, who will pack them in a moist covering and will never allow them to dry out before dispatch. Point 4: divide when they become overcrowded.

To these hints I might add another. Most lilies dislike what professional gardeners call "movement of air," which in plain English means wind or a draught. I have also discovered by experience that the regal lily, *Lilium regale*, likes growing amongst some covering shelter such as one of the artemisias, I suppose because the foliage gives protection to the young lily growth against late frosts, but also because some plants take kindly to one another in association. Certainly the long white trumpets of the lily look their majestic best emerging above the gray-green cloud of these fluffy, gentle, aromatic herbs.

August is the month to plant the Madonna lily, the *Lilium candidum*, that virginal lily, the flower of the

Annunciation, which flourishes for the cottager and often refuses to flourish in grander gardens. Never having grown it successfully, I am the last person to preach about it, and my remarks must be taken as theoretical.

> *Where did Gabriel get a lily*
> *In the month of March?*

I once read, and have never forgotten, those two lines in a poem by Grace James. Wherever that bright Archangel found his lily, it was certainly not in the more ambitious sort of garden. It prefers the humbler home. There is an old tradition that the Madonna lily throve best in cottage gardens because the housewife was in the habit of chucking out her pail of soapsuds all over the flower bed. Curiously enough, this tradition is now confirmed by the advice that the young growth of these lilies should be sprayed with a lather of soft soap and water, to prevent the disease called *Botrytis*. Thus do these old-wives' tales sometimes justify themselves.

The Madonna lily should be planted in August. There is a variety called Salonica, because it grows there, which is said to be more resistant to *Botrytis*, but whichever variety you plant, put in the bulbs so shallow as to rest almost on top of the soil, showing their noses. If you bury them too deep they will have to shove themselves up in that wise way that plants have, knowing what suits them even better than we know, but this is giving them a lot of trouble and struggle which you might have spared them. So plant them shallow, and plant them as soon as they arrive; don't leave the bulbs lying about to get dry. And once they are planted, leave them alone. Don't dig them up to move them to another place. Let them stay put. They are not modern-minded, wanting to roam about; they are statically minded; they are fond of their home, once you have induced them to take to it.

The Madonna lily is an exception to the general rule that lilies demand plenty of humus. It likes lime, which may take the form of old mortar rubble, and it likes a scratchy soil. The scratchy soil idea confirms the old theory that part of their success in cottage gardens was due to the fact that the grit from the surface of the lanes blew over the hedge and worked its way into the ground. Even today, when few country lanes are tarred, this may still hold good, and I have known cottagers send out their little boys with a shovel and a box mounted on old pram wheels to collect grit for the garden. It is never wise to disregard the sagacity of those who do not learn their lore from books.

Blue pool of lobelia

I SHOULD LIKE to put in a good word for the lobelia, dear to the heart of some suburban and most municipal gardeners, but despised by those who pride themselves on a more advanced taste. The poor lobelia has suffered terribly and most unjustly from its traditional use and from association. Association has been the worst enemy of many plants. I suppose that the first time anybody saw pink tulips coming up through forget-me-nots they may have exclaimed in delight. Similarly, the Victorian-Edwardian combination of lobelia and sweet alyssum may once have given pleasure. No longer now.

But listen. Can you discard all your preconceived ideas and think of the lobelia as though you had never seen it before? What a fine blue, as good as a gentian, is it not? And so dense, so compact, such a rug, such a closely woven carpet, you could put a pin though not a finger into the mat of flower. Think of it in this way, and you will instantly begin to see it in a different light and full of different possibilities.

Think of it as a great blue pool. Think of it in terms of waves and washes; think of it in terms of the Mediterranean at its best; think of it in spreads and sweeps and wapentakes and sokes and bailiwicks and tithings. Or, if you have not quite so much space at your disposal, do at least plant it in really generous patches, not just as an edging, and remember the variety called Cambridge Blue, which lives up to its name.

If you must have it as an edging, and if you must combine it with alyssum, try it with the alyssums called Violet Queen or Royal Carpet, instead of the traditional white. The blue of the lobelia mixes into something very sumptuous with their mauves and purples. And I did observe an amusing and original use of lobelia last summer. The dark blue and the bright blue were planted in neat squares up either side of a narrow path leading from the garden gate to the front door. It was like a slice of chessboard, an Oxford and Cambridge chess-board.

Have I said enough to obtain for lobelia a more kindly treatment? It is such an old friend to our gardens. It came

to us two hundred years ago, in 1752, from the Cape of
Good Hope, and it received its name in honor of a bot-
anist who worked here much longer ago than that,
Mathias de l'Obel, physician to King James I. A romantic
story; so romantic that I think our lobelias deserve to be
grown with more imagination than is usually vouchsafed
them.

The advantages of a thicket

AMERICANS MUST BE far more brotherly-hearted
than we are, for they do not seem to mind being over-
looked. They have no sense of private enclosure. They
never plant hedges to cut themselves off from the gaze of
the passerby, nor do they plant hedges between their own
garden and their neighbor's. All is open. Walk in, walk in!
they seem to say, in cordial invitation. Perhaps we should
emulate their democratic spirit, but I doubt if we ever
shall. It is entirely at variance with our traditional idea
that our own bit of ground surrounding our house, our
home, be it large or small, is sacred to ourselves. Whatever our American friends may do, we shall continue to
plant a hedge to block our immediate neighbors out.

An acquaintance of mine has gone a step further. Instead of planting a mere hedge, she is planting what she is
pleased to call a thicket. This seems to me a very useful
idea for anybody who has got a bit of waste ground to fill,
between his own land and the road, or between his own

land and the next man's or just a bit he wants to cram with flowering shrubs and flowering trees which would find no place elsewhere. Thickets can be planted anywhere, can be of any shape, and can be composed of any plants to your choice. If I had room for a thicket myself and had enough span of life to look forward to it twenty years hence, I know what I should do: I should plant it far too thickly and extravagantly to start with, and then should thin it gradually as my shrubs and trees developed in size, crowding one another out; I should eliminate all the ones I liked least, replacing them from time to time with something I liked better, as my taste and knowledge increased. This would be one of the many advantages offered by a thicket: you could remove, and add, and alter, indefinitely. There would be no end to the fun and interest and variety.

Then I should underplant my thicket with bulbs, not only with the obvious daffodils, but also with the many lilies that would enjoy the protection of shrubs, the wind-break that many lilies require. The thicket offers many possibilities. I wish I had one; but the best I can do is to offer the idea to others.

Roses with a touch of romance

DEAD-HEADING THE ROSES on a summer evening is an occupation to carry us back into a calmer age and a different century. Queen Victoria might still be on the throne. All is quiet in the garden; the paths are pale; our silent satellite steals up the sky; even the airplanes have gone to roost and our own nerves have ceased to twangle. There is no sound except the hoot of an owl, and the rhythmic snip-snip of our own pruning shears, cutting the dead heads off, back to a new bud, to provoke new growth for the immediate future.

A pleasurable occupation for us, when we have the time to spare, it must be even more pleasurable to the roses. They get relieved of those heavy rain-sodden lumps of spent flowers which are no good to themselves or to anyone else. There is something satisfying in the thought that we are doing good both to our rose bushes and to ourselves in our snip-snip back towards the young shoot longing to develop, and something most gratifying in watching the pale green shoot lengthening inch by inch in a surprisingly short time.

The shrubby roses have lasted longer than usual this year, presumably because no hot days have burnt them up, but they are rapidly going over and their short season is a thing of the past. I notice that the *Rosa alba* known as Great Maiden's Blush holds her flowers longer than most. This is a very beautiful old rose, many-petaled, of an exquisite shell pink clustering among the gray-green foliage, extremely sweet scented, and for every reason perfect for filling a squat bowl indoors. In the garden she is not squat at all, growing six to seven feet high and wide in proportion, thus demanding a good deal of room, perhaps too much in a small border but lovely and reliable to fill a stray corner.

All the old roses have a touch of romance about them;

the Great Maiden's Blush has more than a touch of romance in her various names alone. She has also been called *La Séduisante,* and *Cuisse de Nymphe* or the Nymph's Thigh. When she blushed a particularly deep pink, she was called *Cuisse de Nymphe émue.* I will not insult the French language by attempting to translate this highly expressive name. I would suggest only that Cyrano de Bergerac would have appreciated the implication, and that any young couple with an immature garden and an even more immature pram-age daughter might well plant the Great Maiden, alias *La Séduisante.*

A ribbon of a path

THE NEW, SMALL GARDEN often presents something of a problem. The owner, or tenant, is usually in a hurry to produce an immediate effect, which is humanly understandable but is bad gardening, since good gardening is a matter of infinite patience. I saw recently a photograph of a back garden in a town, or it may have been a housing development, which seemed to offer a charming solution.

The center of the plot was a grass lawn, and up one side of it ran a path, curving round at the top to give access to the door of the house. This may sound obvious, but the whole point lay in the way this ribbon of a path was designed. It was in five strips; the two outer strips, which might have been two feet wide each, were beds

thickly planted with pinks, pansies, and similar low-growing clumpy things. Inside these beds came two strips of
crazy paving, not very crazy, but fairly regular small
slabs of stone or it might have been home-made concrete.
These two strips of pathway were divided right down
the middle by another bed, narrower than the outer ones,
perhaps only a foot wide, which in its turn was filled with
other low-growing clumps. Sweet alyssum recognizably,
and some tufts of thrift at intervals, and some sowings
of annuals which might have been ageratum and verbena
and the dwarf *Phlox drummondii*, and perhaps nemesia to
give a little extra height. The whole effect must have been
very gay, and very simple and quick to produce with a
dozen seed-packets, a sort of straight river flowing with
brilliant color. Once the initial labor and cost of making
the paved path had been overcome, and once the beds had
been dug and properly enriched with good soil, it must
have been easy enough to keep going from year to year.

Foliage plants

THE EXPRESSION *foliage plants* carries something of
a Victorian sound for us, like the echoing of a gong
through a linoleumed, lincrustaed boarding house, but in
spite of this grim association some of the foliage plants
hold a high decorative value in the garden. They fill up
gaps in the border, and richly deserve to be called handsome.

I am thinking in particular of the acanthus. This is a plant with a classical tradition, for it provided Greek architects with the design for the Corinthian capital to their columns. The form of acanthus they used must have been *Acanthus spinosus*, or *spinosissimus*, which has dark green leaves and a most prickly spike of pale purple bracts, at least eighteen inches in length, showy in July. For some odd reason it is popularly known as bear's breeches, though I should be sorry for any bear that had to wear them.

The form called *Acanthus mollis*, or *mollis latifolius*, has soft, rounded leaves of a paler green. It is less vicious than the spiny one, but on the whole I like the spiny one better.

Natives of the Mediterranean region, they naturally prefer a sunny place, but they will put up with a certain amount of shade. One is always grateful to plants that will consent to grow in that awkward corner where the sun penetrates only for a few hours during the day. Another obliging characteristic of the acanthus is that it will do very well as a plant in tubs or big pots, which you can stand about at your pleasure wherever you need them, on paths, or on steps, or on a terrace, or on any angle that the design of your garden suggests.

If you don't take kindly to my recommendation of the acanthus will you consider the *Funkia* or *Hosta*, the plantain lily? This is another foliage plant, with large gray-green leaves and a spike of green-white flowers in July. It prefers a damp situation, but will grow anywhere you ask it to. It took me years of gardening to appreciate the pale beauty of its leaves and flowers, but now that I have learnt to look at them in the right way I can begin to see what other gardeners meant when they extolled the merits of the *Funkia*.

One has a lot, an endless lot, to learn when one sets out to be a gardener.

Landscape gardening on a small scale

BY MIDSUMMER, most of our plants have grown into their full summer masses, and this is the moment when the discerning gardener goes round not only with his notebook but also with his pruning shears and with that invaluable instrument on a pole eight feet long, terminated by a parrot's beak, which will hook down and sever any unwanted twig as easily as crooking your finger.

A bit of judicious cutting, snipping, and chopping here and there will often make the whole difference. It may expose an aspect never noticed before, because overhanging branches had obscured it. It may reveal a colored clump in the distance, hitherto hidden behind some overgrown bush of thorn or other unwanted rubbish. It is like being a landscape gardener on a small scale—and what gardener can afford to garden on the grand scale nowadays? It must also be like being a painter, giving the final touches to his canvas: putting just a dash of blue or yellow or red where it is wanted to complete the picture and to make it come together in a satisfactory whole.

This is the chance and the opportunity for the good gardener to go round his garden and make his notes for his future planting. He will observe gaps, and will ask himself how he is to fill those gaps up by new plants in the autumn. He will look through catalogs and will order plants recklessly.

Gardening is largely a question of mixing one sort of plant with another sort of plant, and of seeing how they marry happily together; and if you see that they don't marry happily, then you must hoick one of them out and be quite ruthless about it.

That is the only way to garden; and that is why I advise every gardener to go round his garden now—and make notes of what he thinks he ought to remove and of what he wants to plant later on.

The true gardener must be brutal, and imaginative for the future.

The imperial Chinese bellflower

AN EFFECTIVE SPLASH of truly imperial purple may be had in the July-August border with a group of the Chinese bellflower, *Platycodon grandiflorum*. It may be raised from seed sown in spring, though, being a herbaceous perennial, it cannot be expected to flower during the first summer of its life.

The bellflower, or balloon-flower as it is sometimes called, resembles a campanula of a singularly rich color, and does, in fact, belong to the same botanical family. Its shape charms me, when it first appears as a five-sided bud

like a tiny lantern, as tightly closed as though its little
seams had been stitched together, with the further charm
that you can pop it like a fuchsia, if you are so childishly
minded. This, I need hardly say, is not good for the eventual flower. Left to its natural development, it expands
into a five-petaled bell of deep violet, so beautifully veined
that it is worth holding a single bloom up to the light, for
it is one of those blooms which repay a close examination,
revealing not only the delicate veining but also the pale
stamens grouped round the sapphire blue of the pistil.
Such examination may be a private pleasure, and is unlikely to be the principal reason for which we grow this
sumptuous alien from China and Manchuria. It is for the
splash in the border that it will be chiefly esteemed, a
value scarcely to be exaggerated. I should like to see it
associated with the feathery spires of *Thalictrum diptero-
carpum*, a meadow rue, the maidenhair-fern-like foliage
and the cloud of innumerable small mauve flowers of the
thalictrum coming up through the greater solidity of the
purple bellflower; but alas, the thalictrum will have nothing to say to me, patiently though I may plant and replant it, so I must content myself with recommending the
idea to other, more fortunate, people.

The bellflower, at any rate, presents no difficulty and
seems completely happy in ordinary soil in the sun, near
the front of the border, for it grows no taller than eighteen
inches to two feet. One can grow a matching pansy or
viola in front of it.

A good word for dill

MAY I PUT IN a good word for dill? It is, I think, extremely pretty, both in the garden and picked for indoors, perhaps especially picked for indoors, where it looks like a very fine golden lace, feathery amongst the heavy flat heads of the yellow yarrow.

Dill, of course, is not an herbaceous plant; it is an annual, but it sows itself so prolifically that one need never bother about its renewal. It sees to that for itself, and comes up year after year where you want it and in many places where you don't. It has many virtues, even if you do not rely upon it "to stay the hiccough, being boiled in wine," or to "hinder witches of their will." Amongst its virtues, apart from its light yellow grace in a mixed bunch of flowers, is the fact that you can use its seeds to flavor vinegar, and for pickling cucumbers. You can also, if you wish, use the young leaves to flavor soups, sauces, and fish. All mothers know about dill-water, but few will want to go to the trouble of preparing that concoction for themselves, so on the whole the most practical use the cook or the housewife will find for this pretty herb lies in the harvest of its seeds, which are indistinguishable from caraway seeds in seed-cake or rolled into scones or into the crust of bread. Once she has got it going in her garden, she need never fear to be short of supply for seed-cake, since one ounce is said to contain over twenty-five thousand seeds; and even if she has got a few seeds left over out of her thousands she can keep them waiting, for they will still be viable after three years.

The correct place for dill is the herb garden, but if you have not got a herb garden it will take a very decorative place in any border. I like muddling things up; and if an herb looks nice in a border, then why not grow it there? Why not grow anything anywhere so long as it looks right where it is? That is, surely, the art of gardening.

By the way, the official botanical name of dill is *Peucedanum graveolens*, for the information of anyone who does not prefer the short monosyllable, as I do.

Bulbs I can't resist

THE BULB CATALOGS arrive by every post, leaving us in a state of confused temptation. It is suitable to remember that today, August 17, is the feast of Saint Hyacinth, who lived in Poland during the thirteenth century, though Saint Hyacinth has nothing to do with the bulbs we are about to order for planting in bowls or outdoors in the garden. It would be far more appropriate to remember the pagan Hyacinthus, the beautiful youth beloved of Apollo, who changed the boy's murdered body into the flower we still call by his name.

In so short a space I can do no more than mention a few of the bulbs I cannot resist. This will just be a personal list representing a personal taste. Taking the tulips first, I like the great yellow Mongolia, and the great white Carrara and Zwannenberg. I like The Bishop, deep violet in color, sturdy and reliable, on a strong stem, tall, coming up year after year. I like all the fantastic Parrot tulips, wild in their coloring, floppy in their growth, not stiff as the Darwins, a tulip to pick for the house rather than to regard as a flower for the garden. Then I like the broken tulips, the Rembrandts, Bizarres, and the Bybloemens, all

in their different feathery stripes and flakes; and I must not omit the early little Couleur Cardinal, which puts up as pretty and neat a chalice of plummy bloom as any ecclesiastic could wish to see. I always think of it as a young nephew of The Bishop, and should like to see them planted together. Nepotism, if you like to call it that. Only they would not flower at the same time.

Leaving the tulips, we come to the narcissi; and here again we find ourselves in a confusion. I cannot here cope with the innumerable sorts, but would like to draw your attention to some of the smaller ones, *Narcissus canaliculatus*, for instance, so sweet-scented, and *N. triandrus albus,* called Angel's Tears; and also to the single jonquil, bright yellow and strong of scent. These are treasures for the appreciative grower.

Please do not forget the fritillaries. They cost so little, and they increase so surprisingly in grass. They sow themselves, appearing in odd corners where they were never planted.

Bringing a summer look into winter

EVERYONE KNOWS that the seeds of hardy annuals may be sown in the open ground in August and September, and that the resultant plants will be sturdier and will come into flower earlier than those we sow in the spring. Dreadful as it is to start looking ahead to next spring already, knowing what we have to endure before it arrives, the wise man will search now through his seed catalogs and order the packets of pretty larkspur, clarkia, godetia, nemophila, scabiosa, viscaria, calendula, and any bright annuals that entice his fancy. There are plenty of them, and as any seedsman's catalog will give an extensive list, there is no need for me to reproduce it here.

Not everyone wants to be bothered with annuals, though we are all faithful to a few favorites, and there is no denying that they do make a lighter and more brilliant show during their short life than many of the more solemn perennials.

So much for annuals sown out of doors, but people with the advantage of even a tiny greenhouse may have a great deal of fun with a few pots of half-hardy annuals sown in August. They bring a summer look into winter. What could be more summer-like than a pot crammed with nemesia, either in separate colors or in that gay mixture we so often see bordering a cottage garden path? Nemesia will give this reward by Christmas or New Year's Day. Ten-week stocks are well known as a winter pot plant. People who are successful with mignonette in the open can grow this delightful, old-fashioned, sentimental, sweet-scented friend, which always looks to me like a miniature forest of spires of dust-devils. It needs a firm soil, and some lime, and sometimes will elude the skill of the most experienced gardener, though it will often flourish in the little plot of the most inexperienced child. It seems to be one of those inexplicably tricky things with minds and prejudices of their own.

I am assured on good authority that the beautiful morning glory, Heavenly Blue, if sown in midsummer, will produce its wealth of blue trumpets indoors in midwinter. Trained up some tall bamboo sticks, twiddling in and out, with its delicate tendrils and its pale, heart-shaped leaves and its amazing azure flowers, it would indeed offer a wonderful summer-sky reminder on a January day.

The family of the sages

THE FAMILY OF the sages is well known both in the kitchen garden and the flower garden. Some are aromatic herbs, scenting the hillsides in the sun of Mediterranean countries, and are associated in our minds with rough paths, goats, and olives. The sage is altogether an amiable plant; indeed, its Latin name, *Salvia*, comes from *salvere*, to save, or heal, and one of its nicknames is *S. salvatrix*, which sounds very reassuring. The common clary, or *S. sclarea*, is also known as clear eye and see bright. The French bestow a very genial personality on clary by calling it simply *toute bonne*, which to me at any rate suggests a rosy old countrywoman in a blue apron.

The kitchen sages make decorative clumps, for they can be had with reddish or variegated leaves as well as the ordinary gray-green. The garden sages are useful for the herbaceous border. I do not mean that half-hardy bedding-out plant beloved of the makers of public gardens, *S. splendens*, which should be forbidden by law to all but the most skilful handlers. I mean such an old favorite as *S. virgata nemerosa*, a three-foot-high bushy grower whose blue-lipped flowers cluster amongst red-violet bracts and have the advantage of lasting a very long time in midsummer. A more recent introduction, not yet so well known as it should be, is *S. haematodes*, greatly to be recommended; it grows about five feet high in a cloud of pale blue rising very happily behind any gray-foliaged plant such as the old English lavender. This salvia grows readily from seed, especially if sown as soon as it ripens, and will in fact produce dozens of seedlings of its own accord. It is good for picking, if you bruise the stems or dip their tips for a few moments into boiling water.

Anybody with the time to spare should grow *S. patens*. It is a nuisance in the same way as a dahlia is a nuisance, because its tubers have to be lifted in autumn, stored in a frost-proof place, started into growth under glass in April, and planted out again at the end of May. The reason for this is not so much the tenderness of the tubers themselves as the risk that a late frost will destroy the young shoots; possibly the use of a cloche or hand-light might obviate this danger. The amazing azure of the flowers, however, compensates for any extra trouble. Like the gentians, they rival the luminosity of the blue bits in a stained-glass window.

Wild sunset colors

WHILE MOTORING AWAY from home, one learns a lot from seeing other people's gardens. On a recent trip there were some roses I saw: Independence, for instance, of a color difficult to describe. The nearest I can get to it is tomato lightly brushed with gray. It might associate well with the coppery Polyantha Fashion, a very effective rose, lacking the subtlety of Independence, but a fine showy thing for a bed and for picking. There is a whole range now of these coppery-orange roses, Catalonia, United Nations, and Opera are all good; and for a fine rich yellow, with a particularly sweet scent, Spun Gold should come as the discovery it was to me. It was a discovery to the present grower, who found it accidentally. By what I can only imagine to be a printer's error, it is accorded only one x for scent in the catalog; in my opinion it deserves three xxx.

There are also the bi-colored roses, yellow on one side of the petal, red orange on the other, making an extraordinarily brilliant effect. They resemble the old briar Austrian Copper, well known to rose-lovers but often their despair, owing to its tendency to black-spot and die-back; and they resemble also that blazing shrub-cum-climber, Réveil Dijonnais, which a gardener-acquaintance of mine firmly calls Revil Die-Johnny. This should be more often planted, for it is extremely showy and goes on flowering at intervals throughout the summer; it suffers, however, from one terrible fault: it fades into a really dreadful sickly mauve, so if you have not the leisure to pick off the dying flowers every morning before breakfast you had better give it a miss.

If, however, you like the bi-colored roses, as I do, and want something more reliable than Austrian Copper in the same coloring please consider planting Sultane and Madame Dieudonné.

I see that this has turned itself into a symphony of all the wild sunset colors, a sort of western sky after a stormy day. The sunset colors are not always very good mixers in a garden, happily though they may consort in the heavens. In a garden they should, I think, be kept apart from the pinks, and be given, if possible, a place to themselves. I know that few gardens nowadays can afford this extravagance of separate space, but I can still imagine a hedged-off enclosure where nothing but the glow of blood-orange-and-yellow roses should have its own way.

Autumn

A welcome brightness

A SPIKE OF THE BRIGHTEST orange caught my eye, half hidden by a clump of Japanese barberry, *Berberis thunbergii*, which had turned very much the same color. They were both of an extraordinary brilliance in the low afternoon sunshine. I could not remember if I had planted them deliberately in juxtaposition, or if they had come together by a fortunate chance. Investigation revealed further spikes: three-sided seed pods cracked wide open to expose the violent clusters of the berries within.

This was our native *Iris foetidissima* in its autumn dress. No one would plant *I. foetidissima* for the sake of its name, which in English is rendered the stinking iris and derives from the unpleasant smell of the leaves if you bruise them. There is, however, no need to bruise leaves, a wanton pastime, and you can call it the gladdon or gladwyn iris if you prefer, or even the roast-beef plant. Some etymologists think that "gladdon" or "gladwyn" are corruptions of "gladiolus," owing to a similarity between the sword-like leaves; but I wish someone would tell me how it got its roast-beef name.

Its flowers, small, and of a dingy mauve, are of no value or charm, nor should we be wise to pick them, because it is for the seed pods that we cherish it. Not that it needs much cherishing; it is even one of those amiable plants that will tolerate shade. Strugglers with shady gardens, or with difficult shaded areas, will doubtless note this point.

The seed pods are for late autumn and winter decoration indoors, for the seeds have the unusual property of not dropping out when the pod bursts open, and will last for a long time in a vase; they look fine, and warm, under a table lamp on a bleak evening. Miss Gertrude Jekyll used to advise hanging the bunch upside down for a bit, to stiffen the stalks; I dare say she was right; she was usually right, and had an experimental mind.

Let me not claim for the gladdon iris that its crop of orange berries makes a subtle bunch or one which would appeal to flower lovers of very delicate taste; it is frankly as coarse as it is showy, and has all the appearance of having been brought in by a pleased child after an afternoon's ramble through the copse. Nevertheless, its brightness is welcome, and its coarseness can be lightened by a few sprays of its companion the barberry.

The French idea of gardening

I HAVE RECENTLY returned from a wandering holiday in southwestern France, and have been observing with interest the French idea of gardening, as compared with our own. I do not mean the grand formal gardens in the style of Le Nôtre, at which the French with their wonderful sense of architectural symmetry excelled, but the public gardens and the efforts of villagers along the roads.

The villagers produce an altogether charming effect,

comparable with our own cottage gardens at home. The village street is lined with pots, standing grouped around the doorways or rising step by step up the outside staircase when there is one, pots filled with pink geraniums, zinnias, begonias, nasturtiums, carnations, marigolds, all mixed and gaudy. Clouds of the Heavenly Blue morning glory drape all the little balconies, and the orange trumpet creepers ramble everywhere. Especially enviable are the ancient bushes of hibiscus, which in the southern sunshine flower far more luxuriantly than with us, both the blue one and the red one, and that pretty creamy one with a whiskery maroon blotch on each flower, which is like a chintz, *Hibiscus syriacus*. They are usually grown as standards, with a huge head smothered in blossom. Nothing could be gayer or lovelier or, in its way, simpler than this garish exuberance of the village street. It is the natural expression of a desire for color, and I wish our own villages would all copy it.

The public gardens, alas, provide a different story, and bear only too distressing a likeness to many of our own municipal layouts. It seems impossible, even in these days, for the professional municipal gardener to get away from the Victorian and Edwardian passion for bedding-out. Why can he not, in this country, take a hint from the London parks, wellnigh irreproachable in the good taste of their flower arrangements? But no. In France he goes just as bad, and just on the same lines. Horrible lozenges and kidney-shaped and shamrock-shaped beds, laboriously filled with scarlet salvia, cannas, coleus, and nameless monstrosities of variegated foliage; regimental edgings of rosettes like flattened artichokes; vast leaves of not-very-happy bananas in the center; and dreadful little conifers stuck meaninglessly about. The French are also very fond of writing the name of the town in lobelia and white alyssum. Such ingenious practices may please children, but they should not please grown-ups.

Nothing but my intense admiration for the incomparable French taste and civilization could provoke such surprise and dismay. It is all very odd, very odd indeed. One is left wondering why.

A ribbon of Alpines

A MOST PLEASING and original suggestion reaches me in a nurseryman's catalog. It is the sort of suggestion which could provide extra color and interest in a small garden, without taking up too much space and without involving too much labor. It is, simply, the idea of growing low Alpines in a narrow border on both sides of the path running from your gate to your door, or, of course, on both sides or even one side of any path you may find suitable.

By "low" Alpines I do not mean those plants which occur only on the lower slopes of mountains, a technical term in horticulture, as opposed to the "high" Alpines. I mean flat-growing; close to the ground; the sorts that make little tufts and squabs and cushions and pools of color when in flower, and neat tight bumps of gray or green when the flowers have gone over. The range of choice is wide. Saxifrages, silene, stonecrops, thrift, acaena, androsace, aubretia in moderation, thyme, *Achillea argentea, Erinus alpinis, Tunica saxifraga, Bellis* Dresden China, sempervivum or houseleeks, some campanulas such as *C. garganica,* so easy and self-sowing—the list is endless, and gives scope for much variety.

I would not restrict it only to the rugs and mats and pillows, but would break its level with some inches of flower stalks, such as the orange Alpine poppy, *Papaver alpinum,* and some violas such as *V. gracilis* or *V. bosnaica,* and some clumps of dianthus such as the Cheddar pink, and even some primroses specially chosen, and any other favorite which may occur to you. This list is not intended to dictate. It is intended only to suggest that a ribbon or band of color, no more than twelve inches wide, might well wend its flat way beside a path in even the most conventional garden.

But if you had a garden on a slope, in a hilly district, what an opportunity would be yours! Then your flat ribbon would become a rill, a rivulet, a beck, a burn, a brook, pouring crookedly downhill between stones towards the trout-stream flowing along the valley at the bottom. I suppose some people do possess gardens like that. Let those fortunate ones take notice, and, dipping an enormous paint brush into the wealth offered by the autumn catalogs, splash its rainbow result wherever their steps may lead them.

Lilacs of loose delicacy

IN THE LAST-MINUTE scramble to order the shrubs we had made a note of in those far-away happy months of May and June, and have since forgotten, let us now remember the Preston lilacs, *Syringa prestoniae*, before it is too late.

I must confess I don't know anything about Miss Isabella Preston of Ottawa, beyond her name and her reputation as a hybridizer of lilies and of lilacs (*syringae*) and the exciting crosses she has made between *Syringa villosa* and *Syringa reflexa*. I wish I did know more. She must be one of those great gardeners, a true specialist devoting a whole life to the job—how enviable a decision to take, how wise to concentrate on one subject and to know everything about it instead of scattering little confetti bits of information over a hundred things. Such thoroughness and such privity of knowledge carry one back to medieval dates when leisure was the norm. I picture Miss Preston to myself as a lady in a big straw hat, going round with a packet of labels, a notebook, and a rabbit's tail tied to a bamboo stick.

Perhaps this is all wrong, but there can be nothing wrong about my impression of Miss Preston's lilacs. Elinor is a most beautiful shrub with tall erect panicles of a deep rose color, opening to a paler shade as is the habit of the whole syringa family. Elinor is the only one I have hitherto grown, and can give a personal testimonial to; but Isabella is well spoken of, and so is Hiawatha, reddish purple to start with, and pale rose to end up.

All the Preston hybrids are said to be strong growers, and are also entirely hardy as one would expect from the harsh climate in which they have been raised. Whether you prefer them to the old garden lilac, in heavy plumes hanging wet with rain, or whether you will reject their looser delicacy in favor of those fat tassels with their faint scent associated with one's childhood, is for you to say.

Simplify

DOWN IN THE West Country stands a castle, savage, remote, barbaric, brooding like a frown across the jade-green water meadows towards the hills of Wales. This castle has always preserved its secretive quality. It is nearly 1000 years old. It has played its part in English history. It comes into Shakespeare, an honor accorded to few private dwellings by our national poet:

How far is it, my lord, to Berkeley now?
I am a stranger here in Gloucestershire,
These high wild hills, and rough uneven ways, . . .

A stranger myself in Gloucestershire, I had been asked by the present owner to discuss with him the redemption of the neglected garden. It is not everyone who can dispose of terraces falling away beneath towering walls and buttresses, apparently constructed of porphyry and gold—such is the nature of the local stone—but the problems of taste and upkeep affect all of us, in castle, manor house, cottage, villa, or bungalow. The problems vary in degree, but in principle are the same. What will look right? What colors will agree with the fabric, be it this ruddy rusty splendor of Berkeley or the raw red brick of the housing development? What shall we avoid, and what select? Harmony must be achieved somehow. And, as a last imperative consideration, what will give least trouble in maintenance?

We have reached the era of simplification in gardening; and, so far as one can ever feel sure about any question of taste, always a dangerous venture, I feel almost sure that we are now traveling along the right lines. We are gradually abolishing the messy little bedding-out system, and are replacing it by generous lawns of our good green turf. We are replacing our bad herbaceous borders, hitherto stuffed with poor specimens of lupine and what-have-you, by flowering shrubs which entail far less work and are far more interesting to grow and to observe.

There was a terrace at Berkeley, under one of the great walls. It was a wide terrace, and it had been used to provide a herbaceous border. In the old days when many gardeners were employed, staking and weeding, it probably made a good effect. Not so today. "Dig it all up," we said. "Scrap it. Simplify. Make a broad green walk, quiet and austere, to be mown once a week. And on no account smother the walls with climbers. Whatever there is must be special and choice. Simplify."

It is a counsel to be applied to all gardens, whether majestic or modest.

Growing fruit trees in pots

THE APPLES ARE RIPENING, and according to the old theory we shake them to hear if the pips rattle, or cut them in half to see if the pips have turned black. To how many of us has it occurred that those pips may be sown in a flower pot, to be grown on into a little fruit-bearing tree for years to come? It might be a nice idea to sow some apple pips in commemoration of a birth or a christening, and to watch the growth of the infant tree keeping pace with the growth of the human infant. This is perhaps not a very serious form of gardening, but it is fun if you have the time to give to it. Nothing could be prettier than a small tree loaded with fruit. A correspondent tells me that after twelve years she picked a whole hundredweight of apples from a seedling she had raised herself; but then, admittedly, she had planted her seedling out: she had not kept it permanently in its pot.

All the same, it is possible to grow fruit trees in pots. Figs do very well. They fruit best when their roots are restricted, so the restriction of a pot is the very thing a fig needs, if it is not to run to leaf instead of to fruit. A pot-grown fig, heavily hung with its fruit among its beautifully shaped leaves, is a thing to stand in summer on a paved path or beside a front door; it is decorative; and you can eat the figs. The hardy grape vines make very good pot plants. A fruiting vine, hung with bunches trained to arch round bamboo sticks stuck into a barrel sawn in half, is as pretty a sight as you could wish to see:

it reminds one of some Italian paintings, and brings a suggestion of Mediterranean countries into our northern land.

Soft fruit can also be grown in pots. It is well known that strawberries can be made to pour out of a barrel pierced with holes all the way up; the small Alpine strawberry looks charming grown in this way. I remember also seeing a red currant, taught to grow as a little standard, about four feet high, with an umbrella-shaped head dripping with the tassels of its bright red beads. I see no reason why this idea should not be extended to the black and the white currants, and to gooseberries, or indeed to anything that will make a woody stem. Raspberries would, of course, have to be trained round bamboo sticks, like the grape vines. There is great scope for inventiveness here; and the only recurrent care would be the renewal of the soil by an annual top dressing, preferably of compost, to ensure that the plant with its limited root-run was not suffering from starvation. Also to see that it did not lack for water: plants in pots dry out very quickly.

A garden well schemed

THE MORE I SEE of other people's gardens the more convinced do I become of the value of good grouping and shapely training. These remarks must necessarily apply most forcibly to gardens of a certain size, where sufficient space is available for large clumps or for large specimens of individual plants, but even in a small garden the spotty effect can be avoided by massing instead of dotting plants here and there.

It is a truly satisfactory thing to see a garden well schemed and wisely planned. Well schemed are the operative words. Every garden, large or small, ought to be planned from the outset, getting its bones, its skeleton,

into the shape that it will preserve all through the year even after the flowers have faded and died away. Then, when all color has gone, is the moment to revise, to make notes for additions, and even to take the mattock for removals. This is gardening on the large scale, not in details. There can be no rules, in so fluid and personal a pursuit, but it is safe to say that a sense of substance and solidity can be achieved only by the presence of an occasional mass breaking the more airy companies of the little flowers.

What this mass shall consist of must depend upon many

things: upon the soil, the aspect, the color of neighboring plants, and above all upon the taste of the owner. I can imagine, for example, a border arranged entirely in purple and mauve—phlox, stocks, pansies, *Clematis jackmanii* trained over low hoops—all planted in bays between great promontories of the plum-colored sumac; but many people, thinking this too mournful, might prefer a scheme in red and gold. It would be equally easy of accomplishment, with a planting of the feathery *Thalictrum glaucum*, gallardias, the flat-headed yellow yarrow, helenium, *Lychnis chalcedonica*, and a host of other ordinary, willing, herbaceous things. In this case, I suppose, the mass would have to be provided by bushes of something like the golden privet or the golden yew, both of which I detest when planted as "specimens" on a lawn, but which in so aureate a border would come into their own.

The possibilities of variation are manifold, but on the main point one must remain adamant: the alternation between color and solidity, decoration and architecture, frivolity and seriousness. Every good garden, large or small, must have some architectural quality about it; and, apart from the all-important question of the general layout, including hedges, the best way to achieve this imperative effect is by massive lumps of planting such as I have suggested.

I wish only that I could practice in my own garden the principles which I so complacently preach.

In favor of the quince

AS AUTUMN BRINGS round the time for planting shrubs, the ornamental quinces should not be forgotten. They may take a little while to get going, but, once they have made a start, they are there for ever, increasing in size and luxuriance from year to year. They need little attention, and will grow almost anywhere, in sun or shade. Although they are usually seen trained against a wall, notably on old farmhouses and cottages, it is not necessary to give them this protection, for they will do equally well grown as loose bushes in the open or in a border, and, indeed, it seems to me that their beauty is enhanced by this liberty offered to their arching sprays. Their fruits, which in autumn are as handsome as their flowers, make excellent jelly; in fact, there is everything to be said in favor of this well-mannered, easygoing, obliging, and pleasantly old-fashionable plant.

The only grievance that people hold against it, for which the poor thing itself is scarcely to be blamed, is its frequent change of name. It started its career as *Pyrus japonica,* and became familiarly known as japonica, which simply means Japanese, and is thus as silly as calling a plant "English" or "French." It then changed to cydonia, meaning quince: *Cydonia japonica,* the Japanese quince. Now we are told to call it *Chaenomeles,* but as I don't know what that means, beyond a vague idea that *chae* means hairy and *meles* means somber or black, and as, furthermore, I am not at all sure how to pronounce it, I think

I shall stick to cydonia, which is in itself a pretty word.*

There are many varieties. There is the old red one, *C. lagenaria*, hard to surpass in richness of color, beautiful against a gray wall or a whitewashed wall, horrible against modern red brick. There is *C. nivalis*, pure white, lovely against any background. There is *C. moerloesii*, or the apple-blossom quince, whose name is enough to suggest its shell-pink coloring. There is Knaphill Scarlet, not scarlet at all but coral red; it goes on flowering at odd moments throughout the summer long after its true flowering season is done. There is *C. cathayensis*, with small flowers succeeded by the biggest green fruits you ever saw—a sight in themselves. Finally, if you want a prostrate kind, there is *C. simonii*, spreading horizontally, with dark red flowers, much to be recommended for a bank or a rock garden.

The tinies of the tulip family

PEOPLE WHO ARE NOT interested in flowers are not interested in flowers. Not only do they not know their names, which is understandable, since we cannot all be gardeners or botanists, but they simply do not know how best to look at them. They go for the effective mass, and are duly impressed, but the finer shades escape and elude

* A correspondent rightly reproves me for ignorance and frivolity. *Chaenomeles*, he says, means "splitting apple," from the Greek *chaineis*, and *melea*, apple. Obviously, he is right, but I still don't like it.

them, and what a loss is theirs. They have yet to learn
that size and ostentation are not everything.

I am thinking in particular of the little tulips, which
should be planted any time up to the middle of October.
They are the tinies of the tulip family; not to be compared in size with the big Darwin tulips, nor even with the
cottage tulips we see flowering in May. One of my favorites in this section is *Tulipa tarda,* sometimes called
Tulipa dasystemon. I can't think how it acquired the
adjective *tarda,* since it is one of the earliest to flower, not
tardy at all. It is only three to five inches high, striped
green on white; very pretty when the flower is tightly
closed, but even prettier when it expands in the sun, and
opens to a flat star-shaped display of its green and white.

Then there is *Tulipa linifolia.* This is a small, brilliantly
scarlet tulip from Bokhara in Central Asia, that romantic
region which few of us have had the chance to visit, a
paradise of wild flowers. *Tulipa linifolia* can be quite
easily grown in gritty soil for preference, or in a sink-
trough garden with good drainage and as much sun-
baking as the climate will allow.

The same remarks apply to the Greek wild tulip, called
T. orphanidea. This is a bronze yellow outside, opening
in the sun to a starry shape which shuts itself up again
after sunset into a pointed bud, waiting only to expand
once more into its morning star of opened petals.

These are both tulips for the person who knows how to
look into them. Other people who want something more
showy in the species range of tulips would be well advised to acquire some bulbs of *T. kaufmanniana,* the so-
called waterlily tulip. To my mind, they look rather

large and vulgar compared with the tinies who have my heart and love; but it would be silly to deny that they have their own beauty, a beauty comparable to the waterlilies from which they take their name.

Long-flowering shrubs

TWO SHRUBS with an amazingly long flowering period are *Colutea arborescens* and *Colutea media,* the bladder sennas. They have been flowering profusely for most of the summer, and were still very decorative in the middle of October. Of the two I prefer the latter. *C. arborescens* has yellow flowers; but although *C. media* is perhaps the more showy, they go very prettily together, seeming to complement one another in their different coloring. Graceful of growth with their long sprays of acacia-like foliage, amusingly hung with the bladders of seed pods which give them their English name, the bright small flowers suggest swarms of winged insects. They are of the easiest possible cultivation, doing best in a sunny place, and having a particular value in that they may be used to clothe a dry bank where few other things would thrive; nor do they object to an impoverished stony soil. They are easy to propagate, either by cuttings or by seed, and they may be kept shapely by pruning in early spring, within a couple of inches of the old wood.

There is also *Colutea orientalis,* which I confess I have never seen. This has the same coppery flowers as *C.*

media, itself a hybrid of *arborescens* and *orientalis,* but is said to be less generous of its flowers and to depend for its charm chiefly on the gray or glaucous quality of its leaf. One might try them all three, especially in a rough place. I know that highbrow gardeners do not consider them as very choice. Does that matter? To my mind they are delicately elegant, and anything which will keep on blooming right into mid-October has my gratitude.

By the way, they are *not* the kind of which you can make senna tea. Children may thus regard them without suspicion and will need little encouragement to pop the seed pods. It is as satisfactory as popping fuchsias.

Good gardeners take trouble

THE MORE I SEE of finely-cared-for gardens, the more do I realize the high importance given to cultivation. The size of the garden has nothing to do with it: twenty acres or one acre or half an acre, it is all the same, so long as the love and knowledge are there.

Most of us amateur gardeners are inclined to stick in a plant all anyhow, and leave it to take its chance, a chance which probably results in death to it and disappointment to us. Good gardeners, the gardeners who know their job, take far more trouble. They prepare the soil first, making it suitable for the plant they wish to put in; and then later on they look after it, caring for it in times of drought, cosseting it along for the first months of its

young life, nourishing it in its middle age, and never neg-
lecting it even when it attains a ripe maturity.

I note, for example, that lawn mowings are not wasted.
They are spread in a thin mulch over beds. Thin, because
if you heap them too thickly they heat; therefore, never
spread them more than two or three inches deep. The
virtue of lawn mowings is threefold: they keep weeds

away, they retain moisture, and they supply humus to the
soil as the green stuff rots down and returns its vegetable
value into the ground it grew from. There is practically
no plant in the garden that will not benefit from this
mulching—flowering shrubs and flowering trees; herbaceous plants in the border; roses; anything and everything. Lilies are an exception.

Any top-dressing in the autumn is of benefit. Leaf mold

and compost. . . . I know that compost is a controversial point. No one, in theory, denies its value; but many people still say that it demands too much trouble and too much labor and time. Well, I know that a *properly* composted heap is a thing I have never yet achieved in my own garden; I have never yet induced my gardener to make one; so who am I to preach? It should be composed of the right ingredients and scientifically constructed in layers like an enormous sandwich; it requires turning and watering and aerating; but as most books on horticulture include instructions, I need not repeat the details here.

Failing compost or leaf mold, a top dressing of bone-meal in autumn is much to be recommended. A few hand-fuls are easy to scatter, and supply a true, slow-acting food rather than a stimulant. Violent stimulants are apt to be dangerous, promoting a soft, quick growth when what the plant needs is a building-up of its underground consti-tution, to take effect not immediately and dramatically, but in months to come.

These are only a few very brief notes on a large subject. The principle, however, is always the same: you cannot expect your soil and your plants to go on giving you of their best if you are not prepared to give some-thing back in return. This is as true of gardens as of human relationships.

Meanwhile, I wish I had a big compost heap to take to pieces now for distribution, in barrow-loads of the richest dark chocolate cake.

Plants that take happily to layering

I SUPPOSE most growers of carnations at one time or another have propagated them by securing their side shoots into a mound of sand with strong hairpins; but it is perhaps not generally realized by the amateur gardener how many shrubs and climbers will lend themselves happily to layering. It is possible to obtain quite a nursery of young, rooted stock in a short time, at no cost and for very little trouble.

Layering can be done at any time, though autumn and spring are the best. More dependable than cuttings, some proportion of which must always fail save in the most expert hands, layers are almost bound to take root. You make a slanting cut in the stem where it is to be inserted into the soil, and then cover it over with earth and hold it down by means of a brick or heavy bit of stone. Best of all is to sink a flower pot filled with good soil and press the layer into that. By this means, when the time comes for the rooted layer to be separated from the parent plant, usually about a year, the pot can be lifted out of the ground with no disturbance to its occupant, a particularly valuable point in the case of plants which resent disturbance, such as the clematis.

Honeysuckles sometimes layer themselves of their own accord, so avail yourselves of the hint if you want to increase your supply. Azaleas can be propagated by layering, but it takes some time to get a young plant of decent size. Sometimes it is not practicable to bend a shoot down

to meet the ground without snapping it off, and this difficulty may be overcome by raising a pot to the required
height, on an old wooden box, for instance, but be careful not to let the pot dry out. This is the easiest method
for propagating magnolias, whose side branches generally
start rather high up the trunk and are apt to be too brittle
to be very flexible.

I think the first shrub to draw my attention to its self-
layering propensity was the allspice, or sweet shrub,
Calycanthus occidentalis and *C. floridus*, botanically related to the wintersweet. This is such a useful thing for a
sunny place, as it starts producing its brown-red flowers in
June and goes on doing so right into September. Of the
two I like *C. occidentalis* the better, because although it is
rather more straggly in its growth than *floridus*, the
flowers are redder and the leaves more aromatic when
crushed. The wood also is extremely aromatic. I do not
know why it should be called allspice, whose proper
name is *Pimenta officinalis*, a greenhouse plant in this
country, whereas the two Americans are hardy in the
open. They like a loamy soil, and I should add the
cautionary remark that they are said to be poisonous to
cattle.

Taming a steep bank

A STEEP BANK is often a problem. Turfed over, it is
difficult to mow; and the time-honored expedient of
pegging rambler roses down it is not very satisfactory

either, since weeds are bound to grow, and the process of getting them out is both slithery and prickly. A good way of overcoming the problem, and at the same time of putting a waste piece of ground to valuable use, is to transform the bank into a series of little terraces, held up by little dry walls of stone with plenty of earth for plants in the crevices. They would not be any higher than a couple of feet. The flat little terraces would form a kind of shelf for growing all kinds of small treasures, and the dry walls would accommodate many plants that love to get their roots into cool soil at the back of stones. It would be an ideal place also for growing things such as lewisias and ramondas, which like to press their rosettes against a wall-face, so that no moisture may settle in their crowns.

It would be necessary of course, both for convenience and for appearance, to build a flight of steps down the center; or, if the bank is long enough, you could have three flights, one in the center and one at each end. These would be dry-walled against the bank at the sides, giving more space for plants; rough steps they would be, with thyme creeping over their treads. To finish off the whole, a narrow paved path should run all along the base; walking along it, you would look down on the first terrace, the second would be almost at eye level, and the third just above most people's heads.

A few points which I am sure are very important. The dry walls must be built on a slight slant, but probably everyone knows that. Then, it is best to set your plants as you build, because that allows you to spread out the roots comfortably, instead of cramming them into a tight fit afterwards. The terraces will give you plenty of opportunity of adding things later on. Finally, and perhaps most important of all, do use *rounded* stones (weathered if possible) and not those angular objects one so often sees in rock gardens, like old teeth, spiky and grinning. I know that for purposes of dry-walling the stones must have at least one fairly flat face, but that is not incompatible with nice rounded corners.

I fear that these suggestions will appeal only to those who live in a stone country, or who have a number of loose stones lying about, or who can afford to buy them.

A truly perpetual rose

A WORD on the Burnet or Scots roses, so incredibly pretty, mottled and marbled, self-colored and two-colored, and moreover so easy to grow. There is no better covering for a dry bank, since they will not only bind it together with their dense root system, but will also run about underground and come up everywhere in a little thorny jungle or thicket, keeping the weeds away. They are also ideal plants for a poor starved soil or for a windy place where taller, less tough things might refuse to survive. Another of their virtues is that they will make a charming low hedge. Their one drawback, which one must admit to be serious, is that they flower only once a year; but their foliage is quite pleasant to the eye, and if they can be given a rough corner, the brevity of their explosion in June may be forgiven them.

There is, however, an exception to this rule of short-lived flowering. Stanwell Perpetual is its name. It is only half a Scot, being a hybrid between a Scot and a Damask, or possibly a Gallica; I like to think it has Gallica blood in it, since France and Scotland have always enjoyed a curious affinity as exemplified by their pepper-pot architecture and by certain phrases which have passed from one language into the other: *Ne vous fachez pas*, dinna fash yoursel'; and as for barley-sugar, or *sucre d'orge*, I could expand into paragraphs over that.

This is by the way. The rose Stanwell Perpetual is what I was writing about. I have become very fond of this modest rose, who truly merits the description *perpetual*. One is apt to overlook her during the great foison of early summer; but now in October, when every chosen flower is precious, I feel grateful to her for offering me her shell-pink, highly scented, patiently produced flowers, delicately doing her job again for my delectation in a glass on my table, and filling my room with such a good smell that it puffs at me as I open the door.

Stanwell Perpetual grows taller than the average Scots rose. It grows four to five feet high. It is, as I have said, a hybrid. It has another name, according to Miss Nancy Lindsay, who is an expert on these old roses, the Victorian Valentine rose. This evokes pictures of old Valentines— but, however that may be, I do urge you to plant Stanwell Perpetual in your garden to give you a reward of picking in October.

Some members of the arbutus family

THE ARBUTUS or strawberry tree is an attractive evergreen of manageable size and accommodating disposition.
True, most varieties object to lime, belonging as they do
to the family of *Ericaceae*, like the heaths and the rhododendrons, but the one called *Arbutus unedo* can be
planted in any reasonable soil.

To enumerate its virtues. It is, as I have said, evergreen.
It has an amusing, shaggy, reddish bark. It can be grown
in the open as a shrub, or trained against a wall, which
perhaps shows off the bark to its fullest advantage, especially if you can place it where the setting sun will strike
on it, as on the trunk of a Scots pine. Its waxy, pinkish-
white flowers, hanging like clusters of tiny bells among the
dark green foliage, are useful for picking until the first
frost of November browns them; a drawback which can
be obviated by a hurried picking when frost threatens.
And, to my mind, its greatest charm is that it bears flower
and fruit at the same time, so that you get the strawberry-
like berries dangling red beneath the pale flowers. These
berries are edible, but I do not recommend them. According to Pliny, who confused it with the real strawberry, the
word *unedo*, from *unum edo*, means "I eat one," thus
indicating that you don't come back for more.

After its virtues, its only fault: it is not hardy enough
for cold districts, or for the north.

There is another arbutus called *A. menziesii*, which is

the noble Madrona tree of California, reaching a height of 100 feet and more in its native home. I doubt if it would ever reach that height in England, though I must admit that the one I planted here in Kent some fifteen years ago is growing with alarming rapidity and has already obscured a ground-floor window; soon it will have attained the next floor, and what do I do then? Let it grow as high as the roof, I suppose, and beyond. Its lovely bark —mahogany color until it starts to peel, revealing an equally lovely olive green underneath—gives me such pleasure that I could never bear to cut it down. Perhaps an exceptionally severe winter will deal with the problem, for it is marked with the dagger of warning, meaning "tender" in the catalogs.

There is also *Arbutus andrachne*, with the characteristic red bark, but this, again, is suitable only for favored regions. On the whole it is safer to stick to *Arbutus unedo*, so rewarding with its green leaves throughout the winter, and so pretty with its waxy racemes and scarlet fruits in autumn.

The pocket-handkerchief garden

HOW MUCH I LONG sometimes for a courtyard flagged with huge gray paving stones. I dream of it at night, and I think of it in the daytime, and I make pictures in my mind, and I know with the reasonable part of myself that never in this life shall I achieve such a thing, but still I continue to envy the fortunate people who live in a stone country. In this courtyard should grow all kinds of low plants between the flags, encouraged to seed themselves freely . . . and just as I had reached this point in my notes the post arrived, with a letter asking if I had ever seen a very small garden entirely paved and allowed to become a rug of flowers?

No, I had not, but I had often thought of it, for it seemed a solution to the recurrent problem of the pocket-handkerchief garden, which is all that many people are now able to enjoy. It would be extremely labor-saving: no mowing, no weeds. And very pretty and original. I foresee two objections: the initial cost of the stones, and the fact that most people do like a bit of green grass. There are, however, some elderly or handicapped people to whom the bit of green grass is more of a worry than a pleasure; and as for the cost of the stone, it is possible to use home-made cement blocks which are much cheaper and which in any case would soon get partially covered over. Lakes of aubretia, bumps of thrift, mattresses of yellow stonecrop, hassocks of pinks, rivulets of violets: you see the idea?

Amongst these essential and fundamental coverings I should plant small treasures. Shall we say as an axiom that a very small garden should have very small things in it? The picture should fit the frame. I should have lots of little bulbs, all the spring-flowering bulbs; then for the later months I should let the pale-blue camassias grow up and some linarias, both pink and purple, such easy things, sowing themselves in every crevice. I could not agree more vigorously with Mr. Haworth-Booth, who said somewhere that every garden should be regarded as a painter's palette, or words to that effect. I may be misquoting him from an unreliable memory, but that is what he meant. Every garden maker should be an artist along his own lines. That is the only possible way to create a garden, irrespective of size or wealth. The tiniest garden is often the loveliest. Look at our cottage gardens, if you need to be convinced.

Shrubs for kind climates

THIS MUST BE a paragraph addressed to those fortunate dwellers in a kind climate, for the flowering tree which caught my fancy last week is marked by one of those ominous little asterisks in nurserymen's catalogs, meaning "not quite hardy." It is *Lagerstroemia indica*, sometimes known as the crape myrtle, though there is nothing crape-like about its fluffy pink, red, or white flowers. I cannot think how it came by so dismal a name. Pride of India is a much better one. It is a gay little tree, said to attain twenty to thirty feet in height, though the specimens I saw growing by the roadside in Italy were not more than ten to twelve feet, just tall enough to enjoy comfortably with a slight raising of the eyes. I recommend it with some diffidence, since I suspect that only an exceptionally sunny summer would bring it to the perfection of its flowering in this country. It could, of course, be grown against a wall, which would give it protection and an extra allowance of sun-baking, instead of as a standard in the open ground. A loamy soil suits it, and it should be pruned during the winter.

Another thing I noted was the Mediterranean heath, *Erica mediterranea,* grown in the unusual form of a standard. This struck me as an amusing way to train a heath, into a neat tall standard instead of a straggly spreading bush. It was not in flower when I saw it, but I could well imagine what it would look like in March and April: a fuzz of pink on the top of a straight pole. somewhat artificial, I admit, but the Italians are an inventive people and enjoy anything in the nature of a joke. I thought that four of these standards, one at each corner of a square flower bed, might look decorative as little sentinels, not taking up much ground space, and agreeably green all the year round, whether in flower or not; or placed at intervals to form a small avenue bordering a path. They would not grow more than four or five feet high.

Erica mediterranea, unlike most of the heaths, does not object to the presence of a little lime in the soil, though naturally its preference is for peat. People whose gardens are on that type of soil could treat the white-flowered tree heath, *Erica arborea,* in a similar way; this grows much taller, even to ten feet where it is happy, but unfortunately it is somewhat tender and should thus be reserved for the warmer climates.

Adding interest to an old hedge

IT OFTEN HAPPENS that an old, rough hedge occurs somewhere in a garden; a hedge which presents a problem. Too heavy a job to grub out, too expensive to replace, and giving no pleasure to the eye, being composed of a thorny rubbishy mixture, usefully dense but unaesthetic. It is possible to add some interest and color by planting climbers to ramble along and over this sort of inherited relic.

Obviously, these climbers will have to be tough. They will have a great deal of competition to put up with, a starved root run, a spiteful host, and a slash of ungentle trimming in the autumn. Yet if you reflect on the survival of such things as the wild honeysuckle and the wild clematis, old man's beard or traveler's joy, in precisely those conditions, you will see that it should not be impossible to devise a collection of slightly more sophisticated trailers to transform the old hedge from a dull thing into a thing garlanded, here and there, with some streaks of beauty.

A rough hedge, as a matter of fact, offers a real opportunity to the enterprising gardener. We should take a hint from nature, and plant such things as normally thrive in such unkind circumstances. The wild honeysuckle suggests the garden varieties of climbing (as opposed to shrubby) honeysuckles; the wild clematis suggests the more tenacious of the garden sorts. I can imagine *Clematis montana*, either the white or the pink, throwing itself like a cloak over the top of the hedge; a single plant of this should cover an area of fifteen feet within a very few years. *Clematis flammula* or *C. paniculata,* white *and* sweet-scented, should do as well, and should not too greatly resent being hacked about when the time comes for the autumnal trimming. Then, remembering how the wild dog-rose flourishes, we should try some rambling roses of the Wichuriana type, Alberic Barbier, creamy; Albertine, a coppery pink; François Juranville, pink-and-tea. One might also try a wistaria. It would be amusing to see some long tassels of wistaria dangling from amongst the common quick or thorn.

I can imagine also our disgraced and discarded old friend, the Virginia creeper, looking very fine in this novel position, or indeed any of the ornamental vines which color well, if you can ensure that the hedge is not trimmed too early.

A knot garden

IN TUDOR TIMES, the knot garden was fashionable. This meant a garden or parterre laid out on geometrical lines, with narrow paths between beds filled with flowers and outlined by little low hedges of some dwarf plant such as edging box or cotton lavender, which would lend themselves to a neat clipping, or by certain clippable herbs such as the shrubby thymes, hyssop, and marjoram. An edging of thrift was also popular, and can be very pretty, both when it is in flower and when it is cushiony green.

The design of the knotted beds could be either simple or complicated; it could wriggle to any extent, as the word "knot" clearly indicates; or it could be straight and severe, according to the taste of the owner. The flowers which filled the beds would necessarily be low growing, not to overtop the little hedges; pansies and daisies come instantly to mind. If flowers were not wanted, the space could be filled in with tiny lawns of turf or camomile.

It occurred to me that the idea might well be adapted to present-day use. We might well consecrate a separate area to the creation of such a garden. I think it should be flat, I mean level, though it need not be large; in fact the bit usually known as "the front garden" would be eminently suitable and might be made to look very charming and unusual, as a change from the customary rose beds or clumps of herbaceous plants. To vary the knots, it would be possible to plant the box or cotton lavender, or whatever you decide on, in the shape of initials, your own or your children's, done in dwarf lavender for instance, closely trimmed, or in the dark green cushions of thrift which so soon join up and make a continuous line. There is scope for ingenuity.

Time to take cuttings

THE TIME HAS COME to bring the tender pot plants under cover for the winter. What a lot of pleasure they have given, throughout the summer months, those pots of the scented ivy-leaf geranium, those pots of the lemon-scented verbena, standing about in a casual way round our front doors or in odd corners of the garden, where you can tweak a leaf off and put it in your pocket or your buttonhole each morning. I wonder why people don't use pot plants more frequently in this country, especially those people who have not a large garden and want to make use of every yard of space, easy to set a pot down on, taking up little room, and giving little trouble apart from watering when the pots threaten to get dry.

Cottage people and people living in rural villages always seem so clever about this sort of thing. They keep plants on their window sills, flourishing for years, without any light or any attention at all, or so it seems. We might all usefully take a tip from the cottagers, and grow more pot plants to set out of doors during the summer months and to bring indoors as soon as frost threatens, and then just to set them down on a window sill in a room warmed by an ordinary fire, enough to keep the frost out.

This is also a suitable time to take cuttings of any favorite shrub to keep up the supply. There is something immensely satisfactory about a nursery of little rooted plants, growing along, waiting to be planted out or given away. They strike most easily in small pots or in a propagating frame, which need be nothing more elaborate than a shallow wooden box with some sheets of glass or a hand-light placed over it until the roots have had time to form. You can save yourselves trouble by getting prepared compost for cuttings, or you can make it for yourselves out of one part loam, two parts peat moss, one part sand. This is especially useful for cuttings to be raised under glass, but you will find that many cuttings will root out of doors, if you set them *very firmly* (this is important) in a shallow trench made by one slice of the spade and filled in with coarse sharp sand. You must not expect every single one of them to respond to this rougher method, but even if you get only twenty-five out of a hundred it is still very much worth while.

And by the way, a bottle of hormone preparation will go a long way towards helping your cuttings to strike the desirable roots.

Blossoms for the bleak months

MAY I REMIND readers about the fall-flowering cherry, *Prunus subhirtella autumnalis?* As the seasons come round one remembers the things one tends in one's ingratitude to forget during the rich months of spring and summer; besides, there are the Christmas presents to think of. This cherry was in full flower in the open during the first fortnight of November; I picked bucketfuls of the long, white sprays; then came two nights of frost on November 15 and 16; the remaining blossom was very literally browned-off; I despaired of getting any more for weeks to come. But ten days later, when the weather had more or less recovered itself, a whole new batch of buds was ready to come out, and I got another bucketful as fresh and white and virgin as anything in May.

By the way, I suppose all those who like to have some

flowers in their rooms even during the bleakest months are familiar with the hint of putting the cut branches, such as the fall-flowering cherry, into almost boiling hot water? It makes them, in the common phrase, "jump to it."

Have I ever mentioned, amongst early flowering shrubs, *Corylopsis paucifolia?* I believe I have, but it will do no harm to put in a reminder. The corylopsis is a little shrub, not more than four or five feet high and about the same in width, gracefully hung with pale yellow flowers along the leafless twigs in spring, a darling of prettiness. *Corylopsis spicata* is much the same, but grows rather taller, up to six feet, and is, if anything, more frost-resistant. They are not particular as to soil, but they do like a sheltered position, if you can give it them, say with a backing of other wind-breaking shrubs against the prevailing wind.

Sparrows. . . . They peck the buds off, so put a bit of old fruit-netting over the plant in October or November when the buds are forming. Sparrows are doing the same to my wintersweet this year, as never before; sheer mischief; an avian form of juvenile delinquency; so take the hint and protect the buds with netting before it is too late.

Poplars make lines of gold overhead

THERE IS MUCH to be said in favor of the poplar. First, it grows so rapidly that if you are out for a quick return on your money you can get it within twelve to fifteen years. (Landlords and farmers please note.) If it is not money you are after, you will have the gratification of supplying some extra beauty to the countryside; and that still means something to some of us, even if we must be counted in a dwindling minority. Secondly, the poplar will grow and thrive, enjoying itself, in wet ground which no hardwood tree such as the oak or beech would have a favorable word to say for. Thirdly, you can get it for nothing. I know it enrages my good friends the nurserymen when I say this; but I do have to consider my more impecunious readers, and so will say boldly that if you thrust a twig or even a big wrist-thick bit of poplar into the ground and stamp it in very tight, it will take root and grow within four or five years into something that already begins to look like a tree. This is the time of year to do it: November, when the leaves have dropped.

There are several different sorts of poplar. There is the black poplar, *Populus nigra*, which, in this country, we generally call the Lombardy poplar, that tall, towering, pointed tree, the most familiar one, but all too rare in our landscape. Then there is the balsam poplar, which smells so good and resinous on a spring breeze, suddenly; a spreading-out tree, not so elegantly shapely as the Lombardy, but with the advantage of the leaf scenting the air, very exciting when you catch it.

A word of warning. Do not plant poplars where their roots can interfere with the foundations of your house or with drains or land-drains or anything else that their roots are liable to heave up. Poplars may make lines of gold overhead but their root system can be very mischievous underneath.

Trees for autumn color

THE RED LEAVES have nearly all gone now. The *Liquidambar* still retains some, in a variegation of red and green; they cling on for so long that they might be glued on. What an amazing sight this sweet gum must be, in its native home of the eastern United States, where it can grow to a height of 150 feet. It must be alarming to come upon, like a giant torch one ought to extinguish, lest it set fire to a whole forest. It was introduced into England so far back as 1683, but has never yet attained a comparable height here, and may confidently be planted as a sort of exclamation mark of autumn's dying farewell, for it grows upright and pointed, like a poplar.

From the shape of its leaf, it might easily be mistaken for a maple, which it is not. I have no great liking for the Japanese maple, *Acer palmatum*, commonly seen, though seldom seen at its best, but there is a Chinese maple which I dearly love, partly for its beautiful orange-brown bark, and chiefly for the autumn color which it holds so long. This is *Acer griseum* which will eventually grow to forty feet in height, but which even in youth makes a most lovely little tree, like a tree in a fairy story, light and delicate, and bronze as the party-shoes of one's childhood.

Both of these I grow, and have been long acquainted with, but I must confess with shame that the red choke-berry was unfamiliar until someone recently brought me a branch. It flamed as red as a cherry. I think it probably ought to be planted in a clump, say half a dozen, for it makes only a little bushy shrub, five to eight feet high, and a single specimen might not do it justice. Of course the snag about all trees or shrubs deliberately planted for autumn color in a country garden is that they are apt to merge with the trees of the woodland or the hedgerows beyond, in rivalry with the beech, the service tree, and even the oaks; but a concentration in a chosen corner will always indicate that they have been put there on purpose.

There are three kinds of chokeberry, and all three are said to color well; their botanical names are *Aronia arbutifolia*, which is the one I saw; *A. melanocarpa*, the black chokeberry, with white flowers and blackish fruits; and *A. prunifolia*.

Si jeunesse savait . . .

HOW OFTEN I REGRET, as surely many amateur gardeners must regret, that I did not know more about the elementary principles of gardening when I first embarked on this enticing but tricky pastime. How many mistakes I could have avoided, and how far smaller could have been the coffer which my gardener now calls the morgue, and which contains a multitude of metal labels representing the plants that have died on us over two decades of years. I suppose, however, that these remarks might apply to the whole of life—*si jeunesse savait*, and so on—and that one must go forward in the spirit of "It's never too late to learn."

One lesson that I have learnt is to plant things well from the start. A good start in life is as important to plants as it is to children: they must develop strong roots in a congenial soil, otherwise they will never make the growth that will serve them richly according to their needs in their adult life. It is important, it is indeed vital, to give a good start to any plant that you are now adding to your garden in this great planting month.

You may be planting some extra roses in this month of November, when roses are usually planted. Let me urge you to plant them with peat moss and a handful of bonemeal mixed in with the peat. I did this last autumn on the recommendation of some rose grower, and the effect on the rootgrowth of my experimental rose bushes was truly surprising to me when I dug them up this autumn to move them to another place. They had made a system of fibrous root such as I had never seen in so short a time. The reason is probably that peat moss retains moisture at the same time as giving good drainage, and that the bone meal supplies nourishment.

It is usually supposed that roses enjoy a clay soil, and this I do believe to be true, having gardened in my early years on the stickiest clay to be found in the Weald of Kent. But what I now also believe to be true is that although some plants such as roses will put up with a most disagreeable soil, they prefer to be treated in a more kindly fashion, having their bed prepared for them, dug out, and filled in with the type of soil they particularly favor. It is no use trying to grow the peat-lovers in an alkaline or chalky soil; everybody knows that, but what everybody does not realize is the enormous advantage to be gained from a thorough initial preparation.

The small greenhouse

THERE IS NO MORE amusing toy for the amateur gardener than a small greenhouse. It need not necessarily be heated, if he can be satisfied with plants that do not dread the frosts of winter but whose fragile petals suffer from the onslaught of heavy rain or hail. Such plants are better grown under the covering of glass, that transparent canopy which admits the light and excludes the unkindly deluge descending from overhead.

Surely many owners of such small greenhouses have turned them into a sort of Alpine house by now, filled with pans of winter-flowering bulbs such as the little crocuses and early irises. There are so many, so easily grown, and so delightful to watch during the dark days. To go into the greenhouse and to see these little exquisite things in full flower on the staging in midwinter takes us in a great stride towards the longed-for spring and bluffs us into believing that the cold, dead months are behind us.

The squat pans stuffed with such treasures should be filled now without delay. Do not make the mistake I made last year of putting in the crocuses too sparsely. I thought they would look nicer if they had more room to develop, but I was wrong. They need to be crammed tight, as tight as can be, bulb touching bulb, like people squeezed together in a crowd. (I am referring, of course, to the species crocus and their hybrids, not to the ordinary garden variety.) The little irises, on the other hand, the *Iris reticulata* for instance, gain by being given enough space to expand their lovely heads in liberty. Their bulbs should not be set nearer than a couple of inches apart.

Forcing lilies of the valley

A TEMPTATION and a suggestion reach me, hand in hand, in the shape of a leaflet about retarded crowns of lily of the valley. If this leaflet did not come from one of the most reliable and reputable of nurserymen I should mistrust it, for it sounds too good to be true. As it is, I accept their word that I can have lilies of the valley in flower within three to four weeks of planting, at any time of the year, including just now when they would come in appropriately for Christmas. It is a real extravagance, because the crowns will just have to be thrown away; it would be no good planting them out as one plants out the bulbs of narcissus and hyacinths, which have been forced.

All that you do is to order the plants and plant them the moment they arrive, without any delay. They do not like to be left lying about, waiting. You can plant them either in a frame, provided that you can keep the night temperature up to the day, which is not easy unless you have bottom heat; or else in pots or in boxes not less than four inches in depth, which means that an ordinary seed-box won't do; or else in bowls put into a warm cupboard of about 60 degrees, if you have such a thing. Keep them in the dark until five or six inches of growth has risen from the crowns; they must not be exposed to strong light until then, and in any case never to the rays of the sun. For the same reasons of warmth and shade, I imagine that they could be successfully started in their boxes, pots, or bowls under the staging of a greenhouse. They must always be kept moist, and the tips of the crowns should not be covered with soil.

Incidentally, late fall is a good time to plant the outdoor lily of the valley. A neighbor of mine, who has wide drifts of them among the azaleas and primulas of his beautiful woodland garden, says that he never *plants* them at all, but just throws them down on the surface with a very light covering of leaf mold, and leaves them to find their own way down into the ground. I have not tried it, but the method certainly works well with him, probably because he has a soft rich spongy soil, intersected by little streams and offering small resistance to the roots as they feel their way about. They have queer habits; I tried to grow them under trees, which is their natural condition, but they seem to prefer coming up in the middle of a stony path. Plants are really most unpredictable.

The ordinary old English lily of the valley has the sweetest scent of all, but the large-flowered variety called Fortin's Giant has its value, because it flowers rather later and thus prolongs the season by about a fortnight.

Winter

Brown blankets covering secret roots

IT IS PLEASANT to see the garden laid to bed for the winter. Brown blankets of earth cover the secret roots. Nothing is seen overground, but a lot is going on underneath in preparation for the spring. It is a good plan, I think, to leave a heavy mulch of fallen leaves over the flowering shrubs instead of sweeping them all away. They serve the double purpose of providing protection against frost and of eventually rotting down into the valuable humus that all plants need. There are leaves and leaves, of course, and not all of them will rot as quickly as others. Oak and beech are the best, to compose into leaf mold in a large square pile; but any leaves will serve as a mulch over beds and borders throughout the hard months to come.

The professional gardener will raise objections. He will tell you that the leaves will "blow all over the place" as soon as a wind gets up. This is true up to a point, but can be prevented by a light scattering of soil or sand over the leaves to hold them down. This sort of objection may often be overcome by the application of some common sense. There are few people more obstinate than the professional or jobbing gardener. Stuck in his ideas, he won't budge.

November and December make a difficult blank time for the gardener. One has to fall back on the berrying plants; and amongst these I would like to recommend the bittersweet, or *Celastrus orbiculatus*. A rampant climber, it will writhe itself up into any old valueless fruit tree, apple or pear, or over the roof of a shed, or over any space not wanted for anything more choice. It is rather a dull green plant during the summer months; you would not notice it then at all; but in the autumn months of October and November it produces its butter-yellow berries which presently break open to show the orange seeds, garish as heraldry, *gules* and *or*, startling to pick for indoors when set in trails against dark wood paneling, but equally lovely against a white-painted wall.

It is a twisting thing. It wriggles itself into corkscrews, not to be disentangled, but this does not matter because it never needs pruning unless you want to keep it under control. My only need has been to haul it down from a tree into which it was growing too vigorously; a young *Prunus*, which would soon have been smothered. Planted at the foot of an old dead or dying tree, it can be left to find its way upwards and hang down in beaded swags, rich for indoor picking, like thousands of tiny hunter's moons coming up over the eastern horizon on a frosty night.

A handy and intimate garden

THINKING BACK over spring and summer seasons, I am reminded of sink or trough gardens. This is one of the handiest and most intimate forms of horticulture, adapted to the large garden or the small, the town garden or the country; and especially to the rheumatic or the sufferers from lumbago, or the merely rather stiff-jointed elderly.

The point is that the sink or trough can be raised to waist level on four little supports of brick or stone, one at each corner, thus obviating all need to stoop and also permitting a close-up view of the small subjects it may have been found desirable to grow. These little things, these precious Alpines, these tiny delicate bulbs, demand to be seen very close, almost through a magnifying glass, if their especial quality is not to be missed. One has to peer right into them. I think the mistake that people often make is to set their sink or trough gardens low on the ground, when half the enjoyment and half the convenience are lost.

For the rest, the old formula holds good: a big hole for drainage, covered over by a large crock or a broken tile; then a layer of crocks all over the bottom; then some rough stuff, such as fibrous leaf mold; then the all-important soil. This will have to depend on what you intend to grow. You may, for instance, wish to grow nothing but scree-loving plants, in which case you will obviously fill up your trough with a gritty mixture; or you may wish to grow the peat-lovers, the lime-haters; and here is one of the great advantages of trough gardening: you can make up the bed to suit any type of plant of your choosing. As a general rule, unless you have anything special in mind, it is safe to say that a good rich mixture of loam, leaf mold, and sharp sand will satisfy most demands. I would implore you, however, to heap the soil bed as high and deep as you can. Sinks, and even troughs, are apt to be shallow, too shallow, so this fault must be corrected by piling up the soil mixture above the edge-level and keeping it in place with little rocks of stone, otherwise it tends to wash away under heavy rain. These little rocks need not look artificial or pretty-pretty; they are there for the functional purpose of holding the soil up, though at the same time they may contribute to the landscape lay-out of so tiny a garden.

Several people have asked me what to do about their trough gardens during the winter. I couldn't care more. This delightful form of gardening in miniature is exposed to horrible dangers from frost, as we learnt to our cost after the hard days of last winter had passed over us. We then realized, perhaps for the first time after a series of relatively mild winters, that 18 to 20 degrees of frost could harden the soil in the sink or trough into something like a block of concrete. No bulb or root will stand that. They must have got squeezed, crushed, and pinched out of existence. It is no good getting cross with them and telling them that in their native Alpine homes they were called upon to endure far harder conditions, and a far lower drop in the thermometer. True enough, but what we tend to forget is that in the mountains a plant has a bottomless root run wriggling its way down between the crevices of the natural rock, as deep as it wants to penetrate into the type of soil it has chosen for its own.

When we transfer Alpine plants into our sinks or troughs, we are bringing them into completely different conditions. We are putting them into a shallow bed, only a few inches in depth, where they have no means of pushing downwards for the protection and sustenance they need. How, then, are we to safeguard our sinks and troughs from the frost which may freeze them into concrete in any cold night now?

I have been trying to think out the common-sensible answer. Common sense usually works as well as any other sort of sense, and common sense in this case seems to dictate that one should pack one's sink with some warm blanketing such as straw, binding it round the edges with stout string. I should then lay a light covering over the top soil when frost threatened to be particularly severe; and should try to remember to remove it in periods of mild or rainy weather, lest it should exclude the light and air which all plants need even as children need love.

I hope my recipe works.

Bulbs for indoors

IN THOUSANDS OF HOMES all up and down the length and across the breadth of the land, the bulbs so lovingly and hopefully set into bowls last September are now being brought out of their dark cupboard under the staircase. The paper-white narcissus and the early Roman hyacinth are already in full bloom, astonishingly scenting a whole room with one little potful. The ordinary hyacinth is beginning to show its big trusses: a clumsy flower, I think, too top-heavy to qualify for grace or beauty, but indispensable for its scent.

These are the earliest, closely to be followed by what-ever narcissi we have chosen to plant. I stick faithfully, year after year, to old King Alfred, Carlton, Fortune, and Soleil d'Or, which has now acquired British national-ity as Sally Door. Not very enterprising of me, perhaps, to be so conservative, but this year, rather belatedly, I have added one bowl of La Riante, much to be recom-mended.

What fun it is to watch the fat, bleached noses horning their way up through the chocolate-brown mold, and to pinch them gently between finger and thumb to feel if the flower bud is forming, and to bring them gradually into the light they must be beginning to desire. Then, though one is naturally impatient to hurry them along, they must be covered for a few days by a sheet of tissue paper or they will turn green too quickly. (Crocuses of course cannot be forced till the very last moment, lest they come up blind; and the little *Iris reticulata*, however deceptively advanced, always refuses to flower until the old year has turned over into the new. The iris will not accept forcing any more than the crocus, but make the most charming of pot plants, and may successfully be planted out into the garden afterwards, to develop into small colonies year after year.) This is one of the many pleasures of growing bulbs for indoors in winter: you gradually acquire a collection of some chosen varieties for permanent grouping in odd corners in the open. Con-trary to the accepted theory, I find that most of them bloom quite happily in their natural season the first year after being tipped out of their pots. They don't take two whole seasons to settle down after the shock of being forced, though after that they gratefully go from strength to strength.

Mid-winter-monath

WE ARE INTO DECEMBER, *Mid-winter-monath* in old Saxon, and what a difficult time it is to produce flowers to fill even a few vases in the house! The fall-flowering cherry, *Prunus subhirtella autumnalis,* is a great stand-by. I have been cutting small branches of it for two weeks past, standing them in water in a warm room, when the green buds surprisingly expand into the white, faintly-scented blossom suggestive of spring. This is a little tree which should be planted in every garden. It doesn't take up much space, and pays a rich dividend for picking in the cold months. Even if frost catches some of the buds, it seems able, valiant little thing that it is, to create a fresh supply.

Then there is *Mahonia bealei,* a prickly berberis-like shrub which throws up spikes of pale lemon-colored flower, scented like lily of the valley. It is not a remarkably pretty plant, not a plant to grow for its beauty, only for the sake of the flower it will give in this dead season, so I would advise sticking it into any spare corner, with a little shelter from other shrubs if possible. It will do well in any ordinary decent soil, and it doesn't mind a bit of shade.

Those are both out-of-door plants, to be grown in any-body's garden. For somebody who has got a greenhouse, slightly heated up to 40 or 50 degrees, just enough to keep the frost out, I would like to recommend the lady-slipper orchid, *Cypripedium insigne*. This really is a worthwhile thing to grow as a pot plant. The flowers, when you cut them, will last for nearly six weeks indoors; possibly not quite so long in a grimy city, but certainly in a clean atmosphere. The type is greenish, with a brown pouch lined with yellow, and there are many attractive hybrids in variations of color. It is a most obliging creature, prac-tically indestructible provided you don't let it get frost-bitten or forget to give it water. It will probably need repotting every three or four years, in a sphagnum com-post which is best bought ready-mixed from a nursery-man.

The self-contained world of bees

HOW AGREEABLE IT IS, in midwinter, to be suddenly reminded of midsummer. As a rule I do not much care for bluebottles, but when I heard one buzzing out of season, on the window pane, it reminded me of bees, making that fat heavy sound, half-somnolent and half-active, which is the very essence of summer. So slight a thing can suffice to carry one away, whether it is a sound, or a smell, or a touch. I listened to my bluebottle and, forgetting the mist creeping coldly up from the valley, I opened a nice little book which told me, amongst other things, about the garden plants especially useful to bees, and instantly the calendar ceased to say December.

This nice little book is written by a very brave lady who stuffs bees by the handful into her stockings in order to test the effect of their stings on her rheumatism. She is also an experienced apiarist, with a bee-walk or avenue of hives of her own. Her advice on what to plant is therefore not to be disregarded. I was interested to see that faithfully she put at the top of her list that charming yellow-and-white dwarf annual, *Limnanthes douglasii*, which should be sown in spring where it is intended to flower, preferably in a sunny place, and used either as an edging plant or a carpeter. Sticking rather closely, but rightly, to the late Miss Eleanour Sinclair Rohde's well-known plan for a bee garden, she favors also anchusa, arabis, aubretia, bergamot, forget-me-nots, crocuses, grape hyacinths, sweet clover, marjoram, mignonette, Michaelmas daisies, catmint, sage, thyme, and wallflowers. Amongst the shrubs she recommends rosemary, lavender, cotoneaster, barberries, and mallows, and, of course, heather if you are so fortunate as to live in heather country; and amongst the trees she mentions the obvious ones: fruit trees, limes, hawthorns, and sycamore.

I loathe bees myself, one single sting sufficing to send me to bed, quite seriously ill, for nearly a week. Yet I must admit to a romantic feeling for this self-contained world of little creatures, with their extraordinary arrangement of a life entirely their own, but, at the same time, dependent upon what we elect to grow for them. We cannot all grow wide acres of clover, nor can we compete with the honey from Mount Hymettus in Greece, which is the best in the world, even better than the heather honey from the Highlands; but we can at least follow the advice given by Mrs. Lisney in *The Bee Walk*.

Christmas presents for gardening friends

CHRISTMAS PRESENTS for gardening friends. People living in towns will presumably be reduced to visiting the nearest florist and will come away with a pot of cyclamen, confident that, if properly treated, the plant will continue to give pleasure for years. May I point out to them that very occasionally you find a *scented* cyclamen? It is worth sniffing round the array in the hope of coming across one with this additional charm.

If, however, you want to give something rather less obvious than a ready-made plant in a pot, why not compose a miniature garden in an Alpine pan? You can furnish this for yourself with suitable small subjects which can be ordered from any appropriate nurseryman, and can safely be planted now or at any time, since they are supplied ex-pots. The *Sedums* or stonecrops, and the *Sempervivums* or houseleeks, are all useful for this purpose, being to all intents and purposes indestructible; but there are lovelier things such as the saxifrages, and the little pink daisies, *Bellis* Dresden China, and the minute blue forget-me-not, *Myosotis rupicola* (or *alpestris*), which make a pretty group, not flowering in time for

Christmas, but a delight to watch for, long after most Christmas presents have been absorbed into daily life.

Ingenuity and imagination can make a very pretty thing out of an Alpine pan. For instance, a few flat stones laid between the plants to divide them, stones an inch or so in width or length; or bulkier stones stuck upright like tiny Dolomites.

Other suggestions. For the country friend: Fertilizers such as bonemeal or manure; or a bale of peat moss. Tools: these are always useful, because tools wear out and have to be replaced. Prepared compost, for seed boxes and many other uses. String, in tarred balls or in spools of green twist. Pruning shears, to carry in the pocket. Knives, pruning, budding, or just a big sharp knife. And finally, for your own children or for your nephews and nieces, a cactus—because they couldn't kill it even if they tried.

Some roses not often seen

AS I AM WRITING two days before Christmas, I thought I would write on the most unsuitable unseasonable subject I could think of: roses. We are under snow, and the very thought of a rose is warming.

This is a note on some roses not often seen. Comtesse du Cayla, a China rose, so red in the stem on young wood as to appear transparent in a bright light; very pointed in the coral-colored bud; very early to flower, continuing to flower throughout the summer until the frosts come; somewhat romantic in her associations, for the lady in whose honor she is named was the mistress of Louis XVIII; altogether a desirable rose, not liable to black spot or mildew; needing little pruning, apart from the removal of wood when it has become too old, say, every two or three years. *Rosa chinensis mutabilis* makes an amusing bush, five to six feet high and correspondingly wide, covered throughout the summer with single flowers in different colors, yellow, dusky red, and coppery, all out at the same time. It is perhaps a trifle tender, and thus a sheltered corner will suit this particular harlequin.

If you want a very vigorous climber, making an incredible length of growth in one season, do try to obtain *Rosa filipes*. It is ideal for growing into an old tree, which it will quickly drape with pale-green dangling trails and clusters of small white yellow-centered flowers. I can only describe the general effect as lacy, with myriads of little golden eyes looking down at you from amongst the lace. This sounds like a fanciful description, of the kind I abhor in other writers on horticultural subjects, but really there are times when one is reduced to such low depths in the struggle to convey the impression one has derived, on some perfect summer evening when everything is breathless, and one just sits, and gazes, and tries to sum up what one is seeing, mixed in with the sounds of a summer night—the young owls hissing in their nest over the cowshed, the bray of a donkey, the plop of an acorn into the pool.

Filipes means thread-like, or with thread-like stems, so perhaps my comparison to lace is not so fanciful, after all. Certainly the reticulation of the long strands overhead, clumped with the white clusters, faintly sweet scented, always makes me think of some frock of faded green, trimmed with Point d'Alençon—or is it Point de Venise that I mean?

Christ's herb

THIS SEEMS A GOOD occasion to mention the Christmas rose, *Helleborus niger*, in high Dutch called Christ's herb, "because it flowereth about the birth of our Lord." Its white flowers are, or should be, already on our tables. There is a variety called *altifolius*, which is considered superior, owing to its longer stalks; but it is often stained with a somewhat dirty pink, and I think the pure white is far lovelier. Christmas roses like a rather moist, semi-shady place in rich soil, though they have no objection to lime; they do not relish disturbance. If you already have old-established clumps, feed them well in early spring with a top dressing of compost or rotted manure, or even a watering of liquid manure, and never let them get too dry in summer. It is perhaps superfluous to say that they should be protected by a cloche when the buds begin to open, not because they are not hardy but because the low-growing flowers get splashed and spoilt by rain and bouncing mud.

The Christmas rose has been for centuries in our gardens. Spenser refers to it in the *Faerie Queene*, and it is described as early as 1597 in his *Herball* by John Gerard, who considered that a purgation of hellebore was "good for mad and furious men." Such a decoction might still come in useful today. Perhaps Gerard was quoting Epictetus, who, writing in the first century A.D., remarks that the more firmly deluded is a madman, the more hellebore he needs. Unfortunately, this serviceable plant is not very cheap to buy, but on the other hand it is a very good investment because, to my positive knowledge, it will endure and even increase in strength for fifty years and more. It is also possible, and not difficult, to grow it from seed, but if you want to do that you should make sure of getting freshly ripened seed, otherwise you may despair of germination after twelve months have gone by and will crossly throw away a pan of perfectly viable seeds which only demanded a little more patience.

The modest Persian cyclamen

I WENT to a Christmas party given by a neighbor of mine, a member of a great hereditary firm of seedsmen, almost feudal in their family tradition. His baptismal name, most appropriate to the season, was Noël. All the things appertaining to a cocktail party were standing about, on tables; but the thing that instantly caught my eye was a pot plant of cyclamen I had not seen for years.

Delicate in its quality, subtle in its scent, which resembles the scent of wood violets, it stood there in a corner by itself, looking so modest and Jane-Austen-like among its far grander companions. It had a freshness and an innocence about it, a sort of adolescent look, rather frightened at finding itself in company of orchids and choice azaleas and glasses filled with champagne cocktails.

It was the little Persian cyclamen, in its original size before it had got "improved" by nurserymen and swollen into its present inflated form. May I here make a protest against the fashion for exaggerating the size of flowers? Bigger, but not thereby better. Those vast begonias; those tree-trunk delphiniums; those mops of chrysanthemums, all those things called *giganteum*—does anyone really like them, except the growers who get the gold medals?

Ah, no, I thought, looking at the little Persian cyclamen, white, pink-tipped, shy, unobtrusive, demure; this is the way I like my flowers to be; not puffed up as though by a pair of bellows; not shouting for praise from gaping admirers.

I have never seen it growing wild in Persia. Apparently it grows wild also in Cyprus and in Rhodes.

I wish it were easier to obtain. You can buy or be given the big cyclamen at any florist's shop, and I am not saying anything against them. They are a wonderful stand-by at this time of the year, and with due care their corms should last year after year, reviving again in July or August to start on their job of flowering once more before next Christmas. But handsome though they are, these big Christmas-present cyclamen, they do not possess the Tom-tit, Jenny-wren, leveret-eared character of the little Persian.

Propagating mistletoe

THERE IS a prevalent idea that only the birds can successfully propagate the mistletoe, by inserting the seed into a crack of the bark in an endeavor to wipe the uncomfortably viscous fluid of the berry off their beaks. There is no doubt that birds do carry the seed in this way, especially the missel-thrush, hence his name; but it is not true that human beings cannot artificially compete. The late Mr. E. A. Bowles gave a detailed description of his own experience, and as his three-volume book, *My Garden in Spring, Summer, Autumn and Winter,* has long been out of print, I will make no apology for pilfering the gist of the information from his pages.

Save the Christmas decorations, he says; or, better still,

get some fresh berries in early spring. These will be less
withered and stand a better chance of germination.
Squeeze the berry until it bursts, and stick the seed to
the underside of a healthy young twig by means of the
natural glue. Stick as many seeds as possible, to ensure a
good percentage of germination, and also to ensure getting more than one plant, necessary for purposes of fertilization; in other words, you won't get berries if you
haven't more than one plant. The best host trees are the
apple and the poplar, though Mr. Bowles claims to have
been very successful also in starting it on hawthorns.
Some people, he says, advocate cutting or scraping the
twig before sticking the seed on to it, but he does not
agree with this: he says he has got the best results from
a healthy shoot with a smooth and clean bark.

After all this, apparently, you have to be very patient.
The infant plant, always assuming that germination has
taken place, will do very little for the first two years of
its life. In its first spring, that is to say a couple of months
after it has been sown, it ought to show a green disc or
finger, and that is all it will do until the following spring,
when the first two leaves ought to appear, and after that
it ought to go on increasing "at a rate of a geometrical
progression," until such time as you can cut your own
berried bunch instead of buying it, to hang over the
dinner table.

It sounds all right and feasible, and would in any case be
an amusing experiment for the amateur with a bit of extra
leisure and an orchard of old apple trees to practice on.
Commercially, it might prove profitable. Our Christmas
mistletoe is quite expensive, and is, I understand, imported

in vast quantities from abroad. Travelers between Calais
and Paris must surely have noticed the lumps and clumps
darkening like magpies' nests the many neglected-looking
strips of trees along the railway line in the North of
France. Perhaps the neglect is deliberate; perhaps they
pay a good dividend.

A garden composition

PLANT ASSOCIATIONS provide one of the most fas-
cinating and amusing sidelines in the formation of any
garden. Perhaps sideline is the wrong word, for as the
designer's ambitions burgeon so does he realize the importance of this element in the creation of his picture;
and what is a garden, in the last resort, but the creation of
a picture or a series of pictures? The fun of this aspect of
gardening is that it adapts itself to any scale, from the
grandiose to the tiny. You get the great gardens, so large
as to form part of the landscape; you get the diminutive
rock garden where a little fringed dianthus may share a
pocket with a dwarf primula in a perfect fragment of
composition.

Sometimes one picks up ideas on holidays abroad when
one may see the native flora disposing itself in its own
chosen way. No way is better, as all walkers over the high
Alpine pastures will agree. I recall especially, on this
northern January morning, a pine-scented wood in the
Dolomites in June where *Clematis alpina* had twisted its

growth upwards through some scrubby trees and hung its pale lilac heads high above the martagon lilies growing in the leafy soil beneath. It made such a natural picture, so right, so suitable, so ordained. I thought then, and I think now, that one might reproduce that arrangement in a corner of one's own garden.

I envisage a raised bank, ideally supported by a low wall. On the top of this bank or shelf, which would give good drainage, you plant rosemary or lavender. (There are lots of different sorts of rosemary and lavender, tall, short, upright, prostrate, dark-flowered, pale-flowered.) Having planted your top shelf with rosemary or lavender, you then plant *Clematis alpina* amongst the bushes and let it ramble horizontally all through them. You also put in some bulbs of *Lilium martagon,* which will enjoy the protection of the rosemary or lavender, and is one of the easiest lilies to grow, and should reappear happily year after year and even increase; it is said that *Lilium martagon* has naturalized itself in some parts of this country, an encouraging bit of news for some of us who find lilies difficult and disappointing.

It is a good plan to place an inverted flower pot, with the bottom removed, over the roots of clematis, as a protection against any breaking of the fibrous roots when forking the bed. So easily done, so fatal in its results. But remember that slugs love hiding-places such as inverted flower pots, and also love the young shoots of clematis, so put down some slug bait at the same time.

Shields of transparent armor

AS A MATTER of principle, I refrain from recommending anything I have not had an opportunity of trying out for myself, but this time I think I will take a chance. It concerns a new type of cloche, made not of glass but of plastic, featherweight to carry, and unbreakable short of dropping a rock on to it. It is obtainable in varying sizes, ready-bound in galvanized metal, with four little metal legs to push into the ground, keeping it tethered and secure, otherwise I can imagine an exaltation of cloches becoming airborne and drifting away across the landscape, pale as cellophane, a ghostly company under a windy moon.

The makers claim that it admits more infra-red light than ordinary glass, and that seedlings of vegetables or flowers will therefore grow quicker and better. This is the orthodox and practical use for it. For my own part I have not been using it for anything so serviceable as, say, an early crop of lettuce, but have set it to protect some half-tender shuddering things which resent a biting wind far more than they resent an honest frost or a blanket of snow. In my experience the cold northeasters cut and sear leaves into a shriveled brown; one longs to wrap one's plants with some form of protection; one puts sacking round them, but no plants really like being smothered for too long under sacking or hessian, deprived of light and air. They cannot breathe. So now I am trying the experiment of these cloches as a defence against withering blasts.

Obviously, owing to their measurements, they can be used only for low-growing shrubs, and my garden begins to resemble an array of midget knights awaiting the onslaught, inside the shields of their transparent armor.

I hope it works. I don't see why it shouldn't. Seedlings of half-hardy annuals should certainly benefit; especially during the dangerous time of mid-May frosts; and in the vegetable garden a row of these cloches should be invaluable. They are easier to move than glass cloches, because they cannot possibly come to pieces as one carries them, shattering into splinters along the garden path.

Seed catalogs are my undoing

JANUARY IS a dead season, when one cannot get out to do anything active in the garden, so one is reduced to studying catalogs under the lamp and thereby being induced to order far more plants or seeds than one ought to.

I have ordered a summer-flowering tamarisk, *Tamarix pentandra*. This will flower in August, I hope, during that month when flowering shrubs are few. We do not grow the tamarisks enough; they are so graceful, so light and buoyant, so feathery, so pretty when smothered in their rose-pink flower. The earlier-flowering one is *Tamarix tetrandra;* it comes out in April to May.

The seed catalogs are my undoing. I have grown wise, after many years of gardening, and no longer order recklessly from wildly alluring descriptions which make every annual sound easy to grow and as brilliant as a film star. I now know that gardening is not like that. Yet I can still be decoyed into ordering some packets of the Roggli Swiss Giant pansies and the Chabaud carnations, having learnt from experience how good and repaying they are. The pansies, if sown in March under glass, will scarcely flower this summer, or at any rate not until September, but twelve months later they should have made fine clumps which will start flowering in May and should continue without remission until the first autumn frosts. The annual carnations, however, if sown in February under glass (a seed box in a frame or under a hand-light) should fill bare patches during the ensuing summer and are as pretty and scented as anyone could desire. They can be had in self-colors, or flaked and striped like the pinks in old flower paintings; with their old-fashionable look they associate perfectly with the Damask and Gallica and Cabbage roses.

"Carnation" is perhaps a misleading term, since to most people, myself included, carnation suggests a greenhouse plant; an expensive buttonhole for a dandy at Ascot. The Chabaud carnations are more like what we think of as our grandmother's pinks.

Please make a point of getting the two strains I have recommended: the Roggli pansies, and the Chabaud carnations, whether annual or perennial. They are by far the best I know.

Growing annuals from seed

AS I PLAN next summer's garden with the catalogs before me, I wish that the half-hardy annuals were less of a nuisance to raise, for they include some of the showiest of their race: the petunias, the zinnias, the portulacas, the dimorphothecas, the nemesias, and the lobelias which can be so effective if properly used, as, alas, they so seldom are. The brief and gaudy blaze produced by the half-hardies enlivens the summer garden, yet if you have not the facilities to start them in heat, which means a warm greenhouse, and then the leisure to prick them off into seed boxes, and then to stand them out in a frame to harden them off, and then to bother about looking after them while they stand waiting to be planted out—well, then you will have to give the half-hardies a miss.

Of course, they can be sown in the open half-way through May, if you don't mind their flowering rather later.

The hardy annuals need no such coddling. They can be sown straight into the open ground in early spring where you intend them to flower, exacting no more than a rigorous, vigorous thinning out of the seedlings as they come up. This sounds very simple, as though you could buy a packet of seed and sow it in drills or circles or patches, as you desire, and leave it to take care of itself. Don't you believe it. Every seedling demands some care from its grower, and in the case of the hardy annuals I would give three cardinal rules. One, break the soil into a light, crumbly tilth, adding some sand if necessary. Two, sow very sparsely. Three, thin out ruthlessly; annuals need space if they are to develop. Further precautions may be left to common sense, such as putting down slug bait and seeing that the little plants don't suffer from drought, an unlikely danger in April or May.

Colored leaves are very useful at this time of year, both to give a little interest in the garden and to pick for indoors. The shield-shaped leaves of *Epimedium*, some of which remain green while others turn bronze or bronze and green, look pretty with the white Christmas roses stuck amongst them; moreover the epimediums are useful in the garden, too, as a low ground-covering which does well in partial shade. Not very particular as to soil, their preference is for loam and a spadeful of peat. I have found also that the barberry *Mahonia aquifolium*, often seen planted in woods as a cover for pheasants, pays a rich dividend just now. Fill a shallow bowl with its reddish, spiny leaves, and stick any oddments amongst them—some stray polyanthus, a sprig of viburnum or witch-hazel, and, a little later on, some golden aconites. It is a plant for a rough corner, where it can be forgotten until wanted. It will tolerate quite dense shade, and will grow practically anywhere.

Tricksy ingenuity with gourds

A LETTER FROM AMERICA reminds me that people who wish to grow the ornamental gourds this summer should order the seeds now. They can be had in a variety of shapes and colors from the great orange pumpkins (*potirons*), so familiar a sight as they lie hugely about in the fields of France, to the little striped white and green, no larger than a tennis ball. They should be grown under the same conditions as the vegetable marrow; picked when ripe; and lightly varnished with Copal varnish to preserve them for indoor amusement throughout the winter.

It appears that there is a Gourd Society in North Carolina. Our American friends never do things by halves; and although their fondness for a tricksy ingenuity may sometimes outrun ours, I thought I might pass on some of their ideas for the benefit of those who have the leisure and the inclination to carry them out. Thus the elongated Dutchman's pipe gourd may be scooped out and transformed into a ladle. The circular, medium-sized kinds may be scooped out likewise and turned into bowls. A pleasant occupation for an invalid, possibly—what an extract from an American catalog calls "Fun for the shut-in."

The supreme example of North Carolinian ingenuity comes from one competitor in the society's exhibition. She had turned a vast pumpkin into a coach for Cinderella, drawn by eight mouse-sized gourds!

More pleasing to our taste, perhaps, is the harvest festival the Gourd Society organizes for the thousands of people who flock to see it. Throughout the summer, members of the society have grown ornamental grasses to mix with their gourds; and this reminds me that I had always wanted to grow a patch of *Phalaris canariensis*, in plain English, canary seed, in my garden, partly for fun, partly because I could then give a dollop of seed to any friend who kept a canary, and partly and principally because this form of shakers or quaking grass, whose "floures do continually tremble and shake, in such sort that it is not possible with the most steadfast hand to hold it from shaking," was called in the first Elizabethan reign, when writers had some sense of vivid naming, the *Petty Panick*. We suffer from so many major panics nowadays that it is comforting to consider a petty one for a change.

Joke plants

AMONGST OTHER SEEDS for spring sowing I ordered a sixpenny packet of *Mimosa pudica*, the humble plant. Most people, including some nurserymen, call it the sensitive plant, a name that should be reserved for *Mimosa sensitiva*, which contradictorily, is less sensitive than *M. pudica*. So humble is the humble plant, so bashful, that a mere touch of the finger or a puff of breath blown across it will cause it to collapse instantly into a woebegone heap, like the once popular Ally Sloper. One grows it purely for the purpose of amusing the children. The normal child, if not an insufferable prig, thoroughly enjoys being unkind to something; so here is a harmless outlet for this instinct in the human young. Shrieks of delight are evoked, enhanced by the sadistic pleasure of doing it over and over again. "Let's go back and see if it has sat up yet." It probably has, for it seems to be endowed with endless patience under such mischievous persecution.

I must admit that I would like to see it in its native home in tropical America, where, I have been told, acres of pigmy forest swoon under the touch of a ruffling breeze. Nominally a perennial there, it is best treated as a half-hardy annual here. This means that we must sow our packet in a pot or a pan under glass or on the window sill of a warm room. By late summer it will have grown up into quite a tall plant about a foot high; and then you may observe that, like most sensitive people, it is not only sensitive but prickly. It develops large spiky thorns, but still retains its shivering fright. It then becomes not only an amusement for children but a symbol for many of our friends.

If these joke plants interest you I have several more in mind. For instance, the dittany, or *Dictamnus fraxinella,* which you can set alight into a blue flame, especially on a warm summer day, without any harm to the plant. The explanation of this apparent miracle is the presence of a volatile oil; but why seek for explanations when you can so easily entertain your young guests?

The marvel of Peru, *Mirabilis jalapa,* is familiarly called four o'clock, because it opens only at tea time and shuts itself up again before breakfast. It is an old-fashioned herbaceous plant, seldom seen now, but quite decorative with its mixed coloring of yellow, white, red, or lilac, sometimes striped and flaked like some carnations. It can be grown as a half-hardy annual from seed sown in spring, and if you want to save the roots you will have to lift them in autumn like a dahlia. It seems simpler to grow it from seed afresh each year.

Then there is the obedient plant, *Physostegia virginiana.*

The form of amusement provided by this object is the readiness of its flowers to remain in any position you choose to push them round the stem. I never could get it to work, until a Scottish friend told me that I did not poosh it hard enough. If you look carefully, you will see that they have a sort of little hinge. A hardy perennial, of stiff habit, it grows about two feet high and flowers at a useful time in late summer. The variety usually offered by nurserymen is called Vivid, but to my mind this is not a very pleasing shade of pink. For those who share my distaste for pink tinged with magenta, there is a white form, *alba*.

Perhaps the oddest plant of all is the monarch of the East, *Sauromatum guttatum*. The name comes from *saurus*, a lizard, and *guttatum* means dotted or spotted. The flower, which resembles an arum lily in shape, is indeed dotted and spotted like some oriental lizards, only in different colors. The monarch rejoices in the decadent livery of green and purple, with purple bruises on the pale green. Its coloring, however, is not the chief queer thing about it. The chief queer thing is the way it will agree to grow. You set the tuber down on a saucer, just like that, plonk! with no soil and no water, and quite soon it will begin to sprout, and within a few weeks will begin to show signs of flowering.

When it has flowered, you should plant the tuber out in a rather damp corner of the garden to let it develop its leaves during the summer. Then in August or September you lift the tuber, dry it off, and eventually put it back into its saucer, when it will perform again, year after year.

Gardening methods of yesterday

THANKS TO THE KINDNESS and courtesy of a correspondent, I have been looking into an old gardening manual, dated 1797. It is most interesting to compare the methods of yesterday with the methods of today. One comes to the conclusion that our predecessors knew almost as much as we do, and that the cultivation of a garden has changed very little in its fundamental wisdom.

We may have advanced in certain scientific aspects, but in the everyday business we should have little to teach our forebears.

They knew about compost, and set great store by it for top-dressing. Their compost was made of fibrous loam, dry leaves, and dung, so evidently they never incorporated green vegetable matter into it as we do today; that is one up for us. They knew about cloche gardening, which they called glasses or bell-glasses, very much the same as we now use in a more extensive and possibly more exact way, but the principle was the same. They knew all about trimming box edging, which should never be allowed to "run up rude." They practiced the arts of grafting and budding, which they called inoculating. The making of hot-beds occupies an important part in their instructions.

For the rest, this very practical book serves only to arouse a furious envy in our breasts. One has the impression of multitudes of under-gardeners and garden boys rushing about with mats to "defend" tender plants against the slightest threat of frost; wheeling apparently unlimited quantities of horse manure about in barrows; and stoking the boilers for acres of greenhouse. Some of the plants mentioned as commonplaces of the garden are likewise calculated to provoke our worst feelings: double wallflowers, double sweet rocket, double sweet William, all rarities now, to be obtained only with difficulty and at a price. And what did they mean, I wonder, by the tree primrose? Perhaps I ought to know, but I don't. It isn't the polyanthus, as I at first thought, because that is listed separately. It sounds exciting, though rather alarming.*

We must take comfort in the pathetic paucity of their flowering shrubs, compared with the wealth we now enjoy. Rhododendrons are not even mentioned; the vast botanical areas of the Himalayas and China had scarcely been touched. On the whole, I thought, in that respect, we score.

I had hoped to pick up some novel ideas, or, rather, some old forgotten ideas to be revived. The only one I found was a way of growing the ornamental gourds in their "numerous different and singular shapes, sizes, colours, stripes, and variegations." Our ancestors trained them up "tall, firm stakes," when they made an agreeable appearance in the months of July, August, and September. Bean-poles, in fact. I can well believe that they made an agreeable and indeed a surprising appearance in the kitchen garden.

* It isn't either. Correspondents have since informed me that it is nothing more esoteric than our old friend the evening primrose, *oenothera biennis*.

Advice about African violets

FREQUENTLY I AM ASKED to write about the *Saintpaulia,* commonly known as the African violet, though it has nothing to do botanically with violets at all and belongs to the same family as the gloxinia. It is certainly one of the loveliest of small pot plants, with its violet-like purplish-blue flowers nestling in quantities among leaves infinitely soft to the touch. It is rarely out of bloom from one year's end to the other; in fact, there is everything to be said for it except that growers cannot agree on the best way to treat it.

Some people say grow your plants in shade underneath a staging; others say keep them under fluorescent lighting. Some say water overhead; others say don't. Some say keep them to themselves, others say mix them with other plants. Some say that they are ideal house plants; others say they need the humidity of a greenhouse. I think it would be a pity to get discouraged by so much contradictory advice; better to sort out the points on which some agreement has been reached.

It is probably safer to grow them in a greenhouse than in a room that is subject to violent fluctuations of temperature; 55 to 65 degrees Fahrenheit will suit them nicely. They prefer a moist atmosphere to an excessively dry one, though in that case I confess I don't see how they can flourish, as they apparently do, in the centrally heated rooms of America, where they have become so much the fashion that *Saintpaulia* clubs are formed and a whole literature has arisen around them. (I can only suppose that, in their highly civilized way, the Americans have evolved some means of humidifying the air.) They dislike draughts, and if they are allowed to catch cold will perish. They are easily propagated, either from seed sown in March on a mixture of sand and peat moss, not covering the seed, or from single leaves on a stalk one inch long, firmly inserted in a box or pan of the same mixture. Do this in March, and pot on into three-inch pots of peat moss, sand, and one part loam. Never over-pot. Like cyclamen, they will do better under constriction. Water sparingly in winter, more generously in summer, when they will also appreciate a little liquid fertilizer. Never over-water, or they will rot: never let them get too dry either, or they will wither, and never allow water to collect on the leaves.

That appears to be the general conclusion, and may I wish you luck with it.

A rose of any other name

FROM TIME TO TIME I receive nurserymen's catalogs from abroad, and although they are not of much practical use, I derive great enjoyment from reading through them. A particularly pleasing one recently arrived from Naples. It contained an appendix giving the English names, for the benefit of English readers, of some common plants, and as most of these names were new to me, I thought I might transcribe them for the pleasure of those gardeners who prefer the English name, however surprising and Neapolitan.

(On second thought, I suspect that some of them might be American.)

Godetia appears in this appendix as Farewell to Spring. It evidently flowers earlier in Naples than it does here. Nigella, which we usually call love-in-a-mist, appears as Lady-in-the-green. Nemophila appears as Baby-blue-eyes. Tithonia becomes the Golden Flower of the Incas. Scabiosa is the Rich Cushion Flower. Phlox is Texas Pride. Foxgloves are Witches' Fingers. Calceolarias are the Old Lady's Wallet. Thunbergia, a greenhouse plant with us, suddenly seems quite easy and homely as Black-eyed Susan. Collinsia, an easy annual, sounds much prettier as Blue-eyed Mary. Physostegia, the obedient plant, takes on a different character when it gets called the False Dragon Head. The Flag of Spain flies very high under so grand a name, until we discover that it means merely the quamoclit, a climbing plant related to the ipomoea which we all grow under the name of morning glory, Heavenly Blue, in our gardens. *Cobaea scandens*, that invaluable annual climber, which will reach to the eaves of the house in the course of one summer, and never stops flowering until the first frosts, is prettily and aptly called Cathedral Bells. A cool greenhouse climber, *Araujia sericofera*, presumably hardy in Southern Italy, is set down as the Cruel Plant, rather unfairly, because, although it is true that it stickily catches unwary moths during the night, it lets them go again in the morning when the sun shines. It is a tease rather than a murderer.

Bocconia cordata figures under its familiar name of the Plume Poppy, which reminds me that I don't believe I have ever recommended this very handsome perennial. It grows about six feet high, and thus should be planted right at the back of the border. From its gray-green, heart-shaped, deeply cut leaves, it throws up a long panicle in an erect spike of straw-colored flower in midsummer, a flower which is capable of variation in color, for I have seen it also in a dusty pink, very beautiful in conjunction with its glaucous leaves. It is a vigorous root-creeper, but I never mind that. One can always pull up the unwanted bits, give them away, or throw them into the compost heap.

The way with cyclamen

IN LATE WINTER people begin to get worried about their pots of cyclamen and how to treat them in the ensuing months. I suppose that everybody knows they ought to be allowed to dry off gradually and not be started into life again until next July or August, but as I was talking the other day to a big commercial grower I thought I might pass on a few of the hints he gave me.

He advised sinking the pots out of doors in a shady place into a bed of peat moss or ashes, to the rim. This, he said, would retain just the right amount of moisture without any need for watering throughout the months when the corm needs to rest.

He does not advise keeping the same corm for more than two or three years. He says that at the end of that time the quality of the flowers begins to deteriorate, although a second-year corm should produce a larger quantity of flower than a first-year corm. I should not mind the diminished size, myself, since whopping ogreish flowers hold no special charm for me, but that is a matter of taste. He recommends sowing seeds in seed boxes in June, which means that the little plants will have reached flowering size in eighteen months. Of course it also means having a warm greenhouse in which to winter them, and not everybody can boast of that. I dare say that some persons could raise them on a window sill in a permanently warm kitchen. It is certainly the most economical way of ensuring a staggered supply, if you can manage it.

My good friend the commercial grower, who, like most true gardeners, is very willing to impart his knowledge, gave me some further tips. Never, he said, pull a yellowing leaf away. In so doing you may strip off a bit of the skin of the corm, and thus do damage. Cut it off with a knife. Don't tug. On the other hand, always pull the flower stalk away vertically should you want to detach it from the corm. I did know that much, though the bit about the leaf was new to me. How ignorant one is, and how much one learns in ten minutes' talk with an expert!

But wise and expert though he is, he has not been able to resolve a question I asked him. Why do some pots of cyclamen go off suddenly, looking miserable and moribund after two days indoors, when other pots kept in exactly the same conditions survive healthily after weeks indoors? He could not answer my query. He just stood surveying his enormous cathedral, roofed by glass and carpeted by thousands of cyclamen, rose red, cherry red, shell pink, orchid mauve, blood red, virginal white, all as healthy as could be, and gave me a pitying smile.

Chincherinchees have their value

PEOPLE WITH generous friends in South Africa may have received just before Christmas a neat, long, narrow wooden box crammed with something that looked like tuberoses. Alas, they were not tuberoses. They were chincherinchees.

They had no scent, though their heavy waxy appearance suggested a scent equal to the tuberose, the gardenia, or the magnolia. A flower ought to smell what it looks like, but the chincherinchee doesn't. They had, however, a certain beauty of shape, once the buds were fully expanded, and they had, above all, the advantage of lasting for anything up to two months in water. Personally, I tired of them long before then, as they became dustier and dustier; I couldn't face the same vase from Christmas, all through Sexagesima and Quinquagesima, and right up to Easter when I hoped to be picking fresher and lovelier things from the open garden. But I do see that chincherinchees have their value for the many people who have to depend on bought flowers which will last a very long time.

It now appears that chincherinchees may be grown in more exacting climates. I have not tried the experiment for myself, so I can only pass on the information given by the nurseryman who supplies the corms. They should be planted in well-dug open ground four inches deep and six inches apart in mid-spring. No cultivation is necessary except to keep free from weed with the hoe. Then, from the middle of August onwards, you may expect to cut spikes of flower in bud; spikes which will go on for ever and ever.

The corms will not go on for ever and ever unless you lift them and store them away from frost in the same way as you would lift dahlias or gladioli. This means a certain amount of trouble which, for my own part, I would not take for the chincherinchee. Other people may think differently.

The chincherinchees, whose real name is *Ornithogalum thyrsoides*, are related to the well-known star of Bethlehem, that charming little green and white flower which can easily become naturalized, even in grass. We ought to plant this far more freely. It is cheap to buy, and provides a quiet little surprise when you detect it flowering in April.

I must admit that the hundred bulbs I planted last year provided so very quiet and sad a little surprise that they never came up at all. Perhaps they need a year or so to settle down. Or perhaps mice ate them.

The perverse behavior of plants

A FRIEND OF MINE reproaches me from time to time for making gardening sound too easy. My optimism, she says, is misleading. Yet I try to avoid recommending "difficult" plants, or at any rate to accompany them always with a warning. The truth is probably that most plants are temperamental, except the weeds, which all appear to be possessed of magnificent constitutions. The mystery of the Madonna lily, for instance, has never been satisfactorily explained. *Daphne mezereum* provides another puzzle: you may observe all the rules, but nothing will make her flourish if she does not intend to do so. Then there is the case of the self-sown seedling, which, sprouting up in apparently impossible conditions, excels in health and vigor anything similar which you may have transplanted with the greatest care into a prepared bed of the most succulent consistency.

In my own garden I have a curious example of the perverse behavior of plants. Two cuttings of a poplar, brought home in a sponge-bag from Morocco, were both struck and planted out at the same time. Same age, same parent, same aspect, same soil; yet, fifteen years later, one is only half the size of the other. Why? I can suppose only that like two children of identical begetting and upbringing, they differ in constitution and character.

It thus becomes evident that gardening, unlike mathematics, is not an exact science. It would be dull if it were. Naturally, there are certain laws whose transgression means disaster: you would not plant an azalea in a chalk pit. I do agree with my friend, however, that writers on gardening very often omit to make some elementary comments, pointing out possible causes of failure. This brings me to two things I wanted to say. The first is about snowdrops. The time to move them, if you wish to do so, is just after they have flowered. (Do not cut off their heads

as they are very generous in seeding themselves.) The second thing is about mice. They eat bulbs, leaving large bare patches where one has planted snowdrops and crocuses. I asked an eminent nurseryman what one could do about this, and he replied that as one soaked peas in red lead before sowing them, he could see no reason why the same procedure should harm bulbs. It would be an experiment worth trying, because there is no doubt that distressing gaps do appear, for which I can find no explanation except mice. Besides, there are tell-tale little holes.

Winter aconite varnished yellow

IS THE WINTER ACONITE too well known to deserve mention? Surely not. We cannot be reminded too often of so dear and early a thing. It started flowering here, in Kent, on January 20; I made a note in my diary. Then frost came, turning it into tiny crystallized apricots, like the preserved fruits one used once to get given for Christmas. They shone; they sparkled in the frost. Then the frost went, and with the thaw they emerged from their rimy sugar coating into their full, smooth, buttercup yellow on a February day with its promise of spring, when the first faint warmth of the sun falls as a surprise upon our naked hands.

I am being strictly correct in comparing the varnished yellow of the winter aconite to our common buttercup, for they both belong to the same botanical order of the *Ranunculaceae.*

The proper name of the winter aconite is *Eranthis. Eranthis hyemalis* is the one usually grown, and its smudge of gold should be good enough for anybody. It has the great advantage of flourishing almost anywhere, in shade or sun, under trees or in the open, and also of producing a generous mustard-and-cress-like crop of self-sown seedlings which you can lift and transplant. It is better to do this than to lift the older plants, for it is one of those home-lovers that likes to stay put, and, indeed, will give of its best only when it has had a couple of years to become established. So do not get impatient with it at first. Give it time.

There are many small early things one could happily associate with it; in fact, I can imagine, and intend to plant, a winter corner, stuffed with little companions all giving their nursery party at the same time: *Narcissus minimus;* the bright blue thimbles of the earliest grape hyacinth, *Muscari azureus;* the delicate spring *Crocus tomasinianus*, who sows himself everywhere, scores of little Thomases all over the place . . . but I must desist.

Reflections on planting

PEOPLE DON'T always realize that there is time in March to plant trees and shrubs, provided you can get them in when the ground is neither frosty nor waterlogged. May I remind you that a shovelful of peat moss chucked into the hole, and well worked in amongst the fibrous roots as you jiggle-joggle the new plant up and down before finally treading it firm, is of enormous value in conserving moisture and in setting up the root system essential to all plant life. This recommendation to use some peat moss applies not only to the peat-lovers such as azaleas, rhododendrons, laurels, and all the ericaceous family of heaths and heathers, but also to things you would not think of, such as roses. Some plants hate lime, but very few plants hate peat moss.

A handful of bonemeal is also helpful.

These reflections on planting led me to remember a small, upright deciduous tree which I don't believe I have mentioned hitherto in these notes. A native of North China, it is called *Xanthoceras sorbifolia*, and it is not my fault if I cannot supply a simpler name in the vernacular. Its habit of upright growth recommends it for small gardens where space is limited, and in May it is a very pretty sight with its many panicles of white flowers rising in stiff vertical terminals amongst the soft green. Related to the horse chestnut, it is perfectly hardy, though a little shelter is perhaps advisable as a protection for the flowers against late frosts; if frost is feared, the flower trusses may be picked, as they lend themselves willingly to indoor forcing.

The spring snowflake, *Leucojum vernum*, which comes into flower early, is worth noticing now with a view to future bulb orders. It is one of those things which repay looking closely into, turning its white, green-tipped bell upwards, as you might turn a child's face upwards by putting your finger under its chin. Any right-minded child would resent and resist; the snowflake has no option. You may then peer into the delicacy of its structure and its markings, always the best way to appreciate the tinies of drooping habit. Not that the snowflake fails to make its own little effect in the garden. It accompanies the snow-drops and the aconites, and thus is welcome on a dreary morning when every harbinger and prophet means the beginning of spring.

Practical note: plant the bulbs early, in September. Do not be disappointed if for the first year they do not do much. They need a year to settle down; so, obviously, you must never disturb them again once you have got them established. They like a bit of shade, so are useful to fill up a shady corner where other bulbs might not flourish.

Cheerful resisters

THE COURAGE of some small and apparently fragile flowers never ceases to amaze me. Here are we humans, red nosed and blue cheeked in the frost and the snow, looking dreadfully plain; but there are the little flowers coming up, as brave and gay as can be, unaffected by snow or frost. The winter aconite is a cheerful resister, coming through the white ground with puffs of snow all over his bright burnished face, none the worse in his late winter beauty, and increasing from self-sown seedlings year after year.

We all grow the Algerian *Iris unguicularis*—and I wish, by the way, that I could find a nurseryman who lists it in separate varieties, for there is no doubt that some clumps flower much earlier than others, and also there is a considerable difference in the color, ranging from the usual pale lavender to a really fine deep purple. I imagine that the explanation lies in their place of origin, for Algeria is not their only native home; they are to be found also in Greece, in Asia Minor, in Syria, and even so far east as the coast of the Black Sea. It is, however, not of this iris that I wished to write, but of the less familiar *Iris histrioides*, which to my mind has many advantages over *I. unguicularis*, or, as most people call it, *stylosa*. It is true that *histrioides* does not give us a prolonged flowering period, but flowers only once, so that we cannot look forward to picking for many weeks in succession. Once we have granted *stylosa* the superiority in this respect, there is nothing but good to say of the brilliantly blue little actor from the north of Asia Minor. For one thing, it blooms before the leaves have come through, and even when the leaves do appear they are far neater than the frankly unsightly muddle which makes us relegate *stylosa* to a hidden corner. For another thing, the cobalt of its petals is intense. The flower is comparatively large, much larger than its relation *I. reticulata*.

If it is happy, in a sunny place with some mortar rubble to provide it with lime, it should increase by means of the offsets which will form round the parent bulb; and as *I. histrioides* is not at all easy to buy, it is advisable to preserve the offsets and grow them on in pots until they attain their flowering size, which may be in a year or two. This sort of gardening demands time and love, I know; but how great is the satisfaction and the reward.

A wint-pring corner

I WISH WE HAD a name for that intermediate season which is neither one thing nor the other, neither winter nor spring. Could we call it wint-pring, which has a good Anglo-Saxon sound about it, and accept it, like marriage, for better or worse?

My wint-pring corner shall be stuffed with every sort of bulb or corm that will flower during those few scanty weeks. The main point is that it shall be really stuffed;

crammed full; packed tight. The winter aconite will flower first, with *Narcissus minimus,* sometimes called *N. asturiensis,* coming up amongst it, and also the sky blue *Muscari azureus.* There will be the spring flowering crocuses; there will be *Iris reticulata,* the ordinary purple and gold sort, and the earlier flowering blue kind called Cantab; and the black-green *Iris tuberosa;* and I might also risk half a dozen *Iris histrioides,* not very reliable but so lovely that it is worth taking a chance.

There will be many miniature daffodils, tiny, exquisite things. There will be some early tulips, such as *Tulipa biflora* and *turkestanica* and *kaufmanniana,* the waterlily tulip. There will be *Scilla biflora;* and as a ground work, to follow after the winter aconites, I shall cram the ground with the Greek *Anemone blanda,* opening her starry blue flower in the rare sun of wint-pring, and with the Italian *Anemone apennina,* who comes a fortnight later and is at her best in April. Terrible spreaders, these anemones; but so blue a carpet may gladly be allowed to spread.

The corner should be cheap to plant; and needs, humbly, only a little patch of ground where you can find one. Let it be in a place which you pass frequently, and can observe from day to day.

Index